The International Library of Sociology

THE ECONOMIC DEVELOPMENT OF THE MIDDLE EAST

Founded by KARL MANNHEIM

The International Library of Sociology

ECONOMICS AND SOCIETY
In 11 Volumes

I	The Danube Basin	*Basch*
II	The Economic Development of the Middle East	*Bonné*
III	Economics of Migration	*Issac*
IV	Economy and Society	*Parsons et al*
V	The History of Economics	*Stark*
VI	The Ideal Foundations of Economic Thought	*Stark*
VII	The Political Element in the Development of Economic Theory	*Myrdal*
VIII	Population Theories and the Economic Interpretation	*Coontz*
IX	The Social Problems of an Industrial Civilization	*Mayo*
X	Studies in Economic Development	*Bonné*
XI	Transitional Economic Systems	*Douglas*

THE ECONOMIC DEVELOPMENT OF THE MIDDLE EAST

An Outline of Planned Reconstruction After the War

by

ALFRED BONNÉ

ROUTLEDGE

Revised edition first published in England, 1945 by
Routledge, Trench, Trubner & Co., Ltd

Reprinted in 1998, 1999
by Routledge
2 Park Square, Milton Park, Abingdon, Oxon, OX14 4RN

Transferred to Digital Printing 2007

British Library Cataloguing in Publication Data
A CIP catalogue record for this book
is available from the British Library

The Economic Development of the Middle East
ISBN 0-415-17525-9
Economics and Society: 11 Volumes
ISBN 0-415-17819-3
The International Library of Sociology: 274 Volumes
ISBN 0-415-17838-X

Publisher's Note
The publisher has gone to great lengths to ensure the quality of this reprint but points out that some imperfections in the original may be apparent

CONTENTS

PAGE

PREFACE xi

CHAP.

I THE ORIENT AND THE WESTERN CONCEPT OF RECONSTRUCTION 1

Issues of reconstruction in countries with a rapid increase of population and a low standard of living—Meaning of the term "economic and collective planning"—Planned development in Oriental countries and its prerequisite conditions

II TRENDS OF POPULATION IN THE MIDDLE EAST . . . 8

Growth of population in Oriental areas compared to Western countries—Birth and death rates—Development of population since 1800—Growth of large towns—Trends of urbanization .

III POPULATION TRENDS AND NATIONAL INCOME 14

Growth of national income in the world—Occupational structure and distribution of national income—Trend of national income in Middle Eastern countries—Prerequisites for economic progress—Lesson of modern population history for Oriental countries

IV MAJOR ECONOMIC AND SOCIAL PROBLEMS IN ORIENTAL COUNTRIES 23

1. EGYPT: Area and density—Position of agriculture—Structure of land ownership—Living standard and health conditions—Industrial development

2. IRAQ: Agriculture and land problems—Industrialization

3. OTHER ORIENTAL COUNTRIES .

V THE STANDARD OF PRODUCTIVITY IN ORIENTAL ECONOMY . 42

1. AGRICULTURAL PRODUCTIVITY IN THE MIDDLE EAST AND ELSEWHERE: Methods of computation—Value of agricultural and pastoral production at international prices—Calculation of net productivity (net output) per male earner and per ha. in Middle Eastern countries

2. INDUSTRIAL PRODUCTIVITY: Comparative data on the level of industrial productivity—Calculation of earners

VI PROGRESS THROUGH PLANNED DEVELOPMENT . . . 52

Means for methodically improving the economic position of Oriental populations: Redistribution of national income—Increase of agricultural production—Change in the ratio of prices between agricultural and industrial goods in favour of the former—Large-scale production of industrial goods—Development of public services (health, education, transport)

1. INCREASED AGRICULTURAL PRODUCTION AND PRODUCTIVITY PER EARNER THROUGH THE INTENSIFICATION OF AGRICULTURE AND THE EXTENSION OF THE LAND UNDER CULTIVATION: Prospects for an increase in consumption of agricultural products—Actual and optimum diet in Middle Eastern countries—Conditions of competition on foreign markets and self-sufficiency for agricultural commodities—Availability of land and labour necessary for the extension of the cultivated area—Calculation of the Middle East population and earners in 1939 and in 1962

2. CHANGE IN THE RATIO OF PRICES BETWEEN AGRICULTURAL AND INDUSTRIAL PRODUCTS IN FAVOUR OF THE FORMER: Agricultural

CHAP. PAGE

earners in 1934–5 and 1962 and the value of their output—The rise in terms of individual purchasing power

3. Large-scale Production of Industrial Goods (Industrialization) including the Provision of Better Housing: The capacity for increasing consumption of manufactured goods—Family expenditure and distribution of the various items of expenditure—Income elasticity—Consumption capacity for household goods in Oriental countries—Consumption capacity for housing—Potential investments in rural and urban building—Share of industrial goods in building investments—Total consumption of industrial goods to be expected: The economic consumption capacity—Power of local industrial production to compete with imports from abroad—The availability of workers and technical staff

4. Development of Transport Systems, Public Services, etc.: *Per capita* figures for surface transport in European and Oriental countries—Incomes of earners in secondary and tertiary occupations in 1934–5 and in 1962

VII The Finance of Planned Development 90

1. The Rôle of Capital in the Development of Backward Territories: Significance of capital goods for the progress of welfare—Comparative data on capital investments in railways, farming and building in Western countries, Egypt and Palestine

2. The Distribution of Capital Investment in the Past in the Opening-up of Oriental Countries

3. The Rôle of Capital in the Opening-up of Oriental Countries in the Future

4. Planned Capital Investment in Agriculture: Total capital investment in agriculture needed by the Oriental countries—Amounts required for the equipment of various types of mixed farms—Evidences and suggestions for improvements in Oriental agriculture (selection of better wheat seeds, introduction of improved dairy cattle, poultry, etc.)

5. Planned Capital Investment in Industry: Sources of the funds needed—Estimates of total needs to be financed by international loans and local savings

6. International Co-operation in Finance: New financial corporations—Regional development bodies

VIII The Position of Palestine 115

Palestine as the country of the Jewish National Home—The main economic features introduced by Jews: The agrarian sector—The industrial sector

IX The Problem of an Oriental Federation. 122

The economic meaning of a federation—Problems of a customs union in the Middle East in view of the differing economic and social levels in Palestine and the neighbouring countries—Importance of Palestine's purchasing power for the production of her neighbours

X Conclusion 129

Recapitulation of principal deductions as to aim of reconstruction policy in the Middle East and the proposed measures to achieve it—Necessity for using war experience in organizing and regulating production and marketing—The impact of industrialization and rationalized agriculture on the Middle East—The importance of the human element in the transformation process

PAGE

Appendix I: The Agricultural Absorptive Capacity of Middle Eastern Countries 134

Density of population and empty areas in Oriental countries—Iraq's settlement potentialities—Population deficiency—Obstacles to progress—Settlement capacity of Syria and the Lebanon—Water problem in Syria and the Lebanon—Absòrptive capacity of other Oriental countries—The irrigation factor—Average yield per ha. of wheat on irrigated and unirrigated land—Value of crops in the Middle East—Relation between density of population and material and cultural progress

Appendix II: List of Development Schemes . . . 152

Appendix III: The Effect of the War on Post-War Finance in the Middle East 156

Index 161

All experience hath shewn that mankind are more disposed to suffer while evils are sufferable, than to right themselves by abolishing the forms to which they are accustomed.

Declaration of Independence

Planting of countries is like planting of woods ; for you must make account to lose almost twenty years' profit and expect your recompense in the end ; for the principal thing that hath been the destruction of most plantations has been the base and hasty drawing of profit in the first years . . .

BACON : *Of Plantations*

LIST OF TABLES

	PAGE
Birth, Death and Birth Surplus Rates in Oriental and Western Countries	9
Growth of Population since 1800	10
Growth of Large Oriental Towns	11
Share of Large-Town Population in Total Population	12
National Income of the Working Population of England, U.S.A., Germany and Japan	14
Purchasing Power of Average Incomes (per head in International Units)	17
National Income Produced per head of Earning Population	18
Some Data on the Economic Development in Oriental Countries	21
Area, Population and Density per sq. km. in Egypt (by Districts)	24
Growth of Crop Area and of Total Population in Egypt	25
Crop Area per head in Egypt between 1886 and 1935	25
The Urbanization of Egypt from 1897 to 1937	27
Distribution of Land-Ownership in Egypt, 1896–1939	28
Cost of Living of a Family of Five in Egypt, 1931	30
Index of Crops in Turkey, Egypt, Syria and Lebanon, 1929–38	43
Net Agricultural and Pastoral Production in Oriental Countries, Valued at International Prices and Net Productivity in Agriculture, 1934–5, in I.U.	44, 45
Net Productivity per Male Earner Occupied in Agriculture	47
Net Output per ha. of Cultivated Land (in I.U.)	47
Industrial Output per Worker (Gross and Net Output)	49
Earners According to Censuses in Oriental Countries	51
Calculation of Earners in Oriental Countries for 1934–5	51
Distribution of Real Income per Capita	53
Actual and Required Number of Livestock in U.S.A.	57
Actual and Optimum Consumption of the Rural Population in Middle East Countries	58
Actual *per capita* Food Consumption in Egypt	59
Export of Agricultural Products from Oriental Countries as Percentage of World Export (1938)	60, 61
Output and Consumption of Agricultural Produce in the Middle East (on the basis of the 1934–5 Crops)	62
Classification of Middle East Land According to Utilization (1939)	63
Assumed Population and Earners in Oriental Countries in 1962	65
Agricultural Earners in 1934–5 and 1962 and their Net Output	68
Agricultural Productivity and Expenditure per Family	69
Percentage of Income spent on Fuel, Clothing, Food and Medicines	70
Percentage of Income Spent on Food in the Different Income Classes in U.S.A. and in Palestine	71, 72
Average Percentage of Family Expenditure and Average Income Elasticity	72
Manufactured Goods Annually Consumed in a Fellahin Household of Five	73
Other Newly-added Items of Consumption	74
Assumed Total Investments in Rural Building, 1943–62 and Annual Average	76
Assumed Investments in Urban Building, 1934–62 and Annual Average	76
Share of Industrial Goods in Building Investments, 1943–62	77
Assumed Rise in Consumption of Industrial Goods, Yearly Average	78
Imports into Egypt in 1913 and 1938	82

PAGE
Railway Lines and Motor Vehicles per 100 sq. kms. and 10,000 persons respectively 85
Earners in Secondary and Tertiary Occupations and their Incomes in 1934–5 and 1962 88
Capital, Excluding Land and National Debt in 1913 (per head, in I.U.) 92
Capital Investments in Egypt in 1937, excluding Land (1937) . 92
Expenditure on Railways in Oriental Countries 93
Capital Investment in the Jewish Sector of Palestine between 1921 and 1940 94
Foreign Capital in Turkey 96
Paid-up Capital and Debentures of Companies operating preponderantly with Foreign Capital in Egypt 96
Number of Fellah Holdings in Egypt 102
Investment Required for the Equipment of Various Types of Mixed Farms 104
Capital Needed for Planned Development and Sources of Finance . 111
Import and Export between Palestine and the Neighbouring Countries, 1931–40 125
Comparative Data on Oriental Economies. 126
Comparative Import and Export Figures for Middle Eastern and Other Countries 127
Approximate Classification of Land Surface in Iraq 137
Area, Population and Density in Syria (1935) 141
Density of Population subsisting on Agriculture per sq. km. of Cultivated Land 145
Average Yield in kg. per hectare of Wheat 147
Value of Crops in the Middle East (Estimates—1937) 148
Density of Rural Population in Oriental Countries per sq. km. of Cultivable Land, 1939 148

TABLE OF WEIGHTS AND MEASURES

AREA

EGYPT: One Feddan = 4,201 square metres = 1·038 acres
PALESTINE: One Dunam (Turkish dunam) = 919·3 square metres
" " (metric dunam) = 1,000 square metres

WEIGHTS

EGYPT: One kantar = 44·9 kg.
One ardeb (of wheat) = 150 kg.
" " (of maize) = 140 kg.

CURRENCY

EGYPT: One Egyptian pound (£E.) = 100 Egyptian piastres
(One pound sterling [£] = 97·5 Egyptian piastres or £E.0·975)
TURKEY: One Turkish pound (LT.) = 100 Turkish piastres
(One pound sterling [£] = 5·22 Turkish pounds—Dec. 1942)
SYRIA: One Syrian Lebanese pound (£LS) = 100 Syrian Lebanese piastres = 20 French francs
(One pound sterling [£] = 8·85 Syr. Leb. pounds—Dec. 1942)
IRAQ: One Iraqi dinar (I.D.) = 1,000 fils (20 dirhams) = one pound sterling
PALESTINE: One Palestine pound (LP.) = 1,000 mils = one pound sterling.

One International Unit (I.U.) = approx. one U.S. Dollar. This unit was introduced by Mr. Colin Clark for the purpose of international comparison (see p. 17).

PREFACE

The Middle East is to an increasing degree becoming part of the international society of nations ; and as such it is being integrated more and more within the framework of modern international economic, social and cultural relations. But it is not so long since the Oriental countries formed a block of their own, bearing the marks of a largely uniform régime and civilization that had a great many national, political and cultural features in common. This joint heritage is still observable to-day in many fields, although the basic political factors which in former times brought about this unity have meanwhile been seriously disturbed.[1]

One of the factors—probably eliminated for good by events since the last war—was the dominant rôle of foreigners and foreign capital in the economic and political life of Middle Eastern countries. There were various reasons, on which there is no need to dwell here, for the growing importance of these foreign influences in recent generations. The problems involved in the transformation of Middle Eastern Society and Economics hitherto are comprehensively treated in my book entitled *State and Economics in the Middle East*, which will appear in the near future.

In recasting the economic life of these regions after the war, it will be impossible to ignore the factors which account for the peculiar development of economic life in the East, and for that distinctive outlook and attitude of the Orient towards economic affairs which has not yet disappeared despite the vast progress seen. It would be a serious mistake if the indiscriminate application of methods, views, measures and the like that have grown up in Western countries were to be recommended for the East as well.

But there is yet another difficulty. In the course of many decades Western countries, large powers as well as small states, have developed comprehensive institutions for the statistical and scientific exploration of almost all aspects and fields of economic and social life. Thus it has become possible to approach problems of planning in the West with measuring rods and instruments that are adapted to their purposes, and to gauge the possibilities and prospects of planned reconstruction with a high degree of

[1] The term "Middle East," as used here, embraces the following Oriental countries: Turkey, Syria and Lebanon, Palestine, Transjordan, Iraq, Egypt, and Cyprus. Iran and the States and dependencies of the Arab Peninsula belong to the same block in a sense, but are not treated in this work as various features common to the other countries are missing.

probability ; for the size of things, their ratio and scope as well as their interrelations, are largely known there. In the East, however, the situation is rather different. Here, it is true, commendable statistical work has already been done, but on a far more limited scale. Thus fundamental types of information, which constitute the backbone of Western statistics, are still lacking in many Oriental countries, with the inevitable result that planning for Oriental regions, with the possible exception of Palestine, can be undertaken only subject to reservations regarding the correctness of those underlying estimates which must be used in lieu of exact data. This fact will have to be borne in mind whenever reconstruction schemes for Eastern and Western countries are compared.

Yet the necessity for preparing material and proposals for reconstruction exists in the East no less than in the West. Hence we must go on working, incomplete and scanty though our data may be, while comforting ourselves with the thought that later on, when a more advanced stage of basic statistical knowledge has been achieved, our results will be improved and amplified.

It is my pleasant duty to thank Dr. Elsa Schächter and Dr. Esther Pines for their valuable help in the preparation of many of the tables contained in this book. I must also express my gratitude to the many friends by whose suggestions and comments I have profited.

Part of Chapters I and II and a section of the Appendix on the Agricultural Absorptive Capacity of the Middle East have already appeared in *L'Egypte Contemporaine* and the monthly *Palestine and the Middle East* respectively, to the editors of which I wish to tender my thanks.

Jerusalem, *July 1943*.

ALFRED BONNÉ.

THE ECONOMIC DEVELOPMENT OF THE MIDDLE EAST

CHAPTER I

THE ORIENT AND THE WESTERN CONCEPT OF RECONSTRUCTION

Any economic and social reorganization of the territories of the Old and the New Worlds must allow for the inescapable fact that the countries linking the continents of Europe, Asia and Africa function at an exceedingly low social and economic level. As long as communications between the various parts of the world and within the Orient itself could be maintained only by dint of great effort, the marked differences between the standards of living of the population of the various countries were not sufficient to provoke social unrest and discontent. The resignation of the inhabitants, the frugality of their lives and their own ignorance of all that was going on beyond their own particular districts prevented them, so to speak, from realizing their hard lot. This fatalistic attitude has gradually altered. Following the political liberation of the peoples of the East from foreign dominion, their sense of economic welfare and independence has been stirred considerably. The linking of even remote regions and localities with centres of trade and communications and with the capitals of their countries, the development of modern means of transport, the dissemination of modern social ideas, have all combined to inculcate new notions of state and society among the under-privileged classes, who form the bulk of the Oriental population. As a result it is incumbent upon the governments of Oriental states to bring their countries into accord with modern social and economic standards, and to devise ways and means for achieving this end. There can be no doubt that such a policy will assume added importance after the present war; the slogans " freedom from want " and " social security ", pointing to the necessity of far-reaching social reforms, are probably nowhere so justified as in the countries of the East.

These are confronted with a number of exceedingly complicated issues. In the first place comes the rapid growth of population. This phenomenon has been operative in Eastern countries for decades. With an annual increase of more than 600,000 persons in Middle East countries alone, it aggravates the problem of existence of the indigenous population in its present form. There are furthermore the vast differences in the material position of the inhabitants, the inadequate general education and the low level of civilization in those countries. Illiteracy is still so widely prevalent that, bearing in mind its restrictive influence on the development of the economic potentialities of the region as a whole, one can hardly expect the population to display much initiative and activity of its own in the near future. Only once in modern times has there been any attempt on the part of a great state to solve problems of such magnitude, namely, the Russian Revolution. The Western world did not approve of the methods used in the course of this experiment; but it does recognize that Russia can teach important lessons when similar problems have to be handled in other countries. On the Twenty-Fourth Anniversary of the Russian Revolution, *The Times* wrote, on the 7th November, 1941, that if the English-speaking democracies justly pride themselves on the establishment of individual freedom and individual worth as the corner-stone of society, they had in recent years come to understand that the freedom of the individual could be made secure only by a measure of that collective planning for social ends which had been the proclaimed ideal of the Soviet order. If the English tradition had in the past dwelt rather on political rights, and the Soviet system on social and economic rights, it might now be recognized on both sides that exclusive concentration either on the one or on the other produces an imperfect society. Similar quotations from no less representative sources could be easily adduced. It therefore appears that collective planning can now be regarded as a key concept for the reshaping of the economic and social destiny of large parts of the world.

A question of major importance is the interpretation of the term "collective planning" and "planned reconstruction". For the purpose of the present study these expressions must be taken in the sense accepted by the leading protagonists of a Planned New Order.

These do not rely on a sudden revolution for achieving those ends, but believe in the possibility of eliminating many of the economic problems and evils of our days, raising the standard of living, preventing the periodic recurrence of unemployment, diseases, etc., by well-planned state intervention. The world does not consider these problems to be insoluble, nor does it regard every approach to them as illusory. Much has, in fact, been achieved since the various movements for the betterment of economic and social conditions first commenced some generations ago; and despite considerable scepticism and deprecatory comments on the unrealistic approach, far-reaching changes have been effected in most countries. The speakers of the New Order, as their positions indicate, are by no means unworldly academicians but leading statesmen and practical economists who have placed themselves at the head of the movement. A characteristic example of this school of thought, which is founded on the belief in a new form of international economic collaboration, is provided in a speech made by Mr. Winant, the American Ambassador in London:

> What we want is not complicated. We have enough technical knowledge and organizing ability to respond to this awakening of social conscience. . . . When war is done, the drive for tanks must become a drive for houses. The drive for food to prevent the enemy from starving us must become a drive for food to satisfy the needs of all people in all countries. The drive for physical fitness in the forces must become a drive for bringing death and sickness rates in the whole population down to the lowest possible level. The drive for man-power in war must become a drive for employment to make freedom from want a living reality. The drive for an all-out war effort by the United Nations must become a drive for an all-out peace effort, based on the same co-operation and willingness to sacrifice.[1]

It is certainly possible to belittle the ideas outlined in such statements as these, in view of the fact that no far-reaching planning policy can be pursued without general consent. But the critics make their task somewhat easy by depicting planned reconstruction as a tremendously complicated issue or a target too lofty for practical men. Certainly, if every detail of private life and work would require to be regimented and planned in advance, the task would be impossible and undesirable. Nor is there any intention here of providing a blue-print for the establishment of a fully socialist economy with all that the latter may imply from the extrusion of the present ruling classes to a full planning of production and consumption. Planned reconstruction has a more modest and immediate meaning. It is to be understood here in the sense of devising and co-ordinating

[1] *The Economist*, No. 5160, July 18, 1942, pp. 66–7.

all measures at the disposal of governments in order to make the best use of a nation's human and material resources for the maximum wealth and welfare of its subjects. There exist, of course, differences in the points of departure and approaches to these objectives on the part of the various sections of the population within one country, and between the various countries themselves. This would not matter so long as certain general implications in the trend of economic and social development of most progressive countries, which can already be traced during recent decades, are definitely acknowledged. Foremost among them comes the need for increasing world productivity and for achieving a more equal distribution of the produced goods. Both ends can be attained without the introduction of a totalitarian economy; yet at the same time the old liberal notion of freedom within the economic sphere will definitely have to be abandoned.

That these are no mere generalizing formulæ is seen from the growing practical preparations for comprehensive reconstruction projects in the Western world and the great importance attached to them by competent and objective observers like Harold Butler, who with all due caution stresses their far-reaching consequences for the future reshaping of world economy:

> Though the thinking which it inspires is necessarily based on American experience and looks first to the solution of American problems, it conceives American prosperity as a condition and as a consequence of a general prosperity diffused over the world. It recognizes that the preponderant economic position of the United States imposes upon it a special responsibility, inasmuch as by its policies the economic and therefore to a large extent the political harmony of the world-community will be determined. At the same time it is also aware that reconstruction cannot be carried out by the United States alone. It involves an extensive system of co-operation with other nations, which cannot be made effective without a great deal of international organization. Accordingly Americans are beginning to look to the adaptation to peace uses of the extensive machinery already created by the United Nations for the successful prosecution of the war. It is safe to assume that all this thinking will not be without practical consequences. To regard it as an interesting intellectual exercise unrelated to future American action would be a dangerous error. . . .[1]

It is not improbable that during the war and the immediate post-war period there may be some changes and modifications

[1] Harold Butler, "The American Approach to Reconstruction," *Agenda*, 1942, p. 104.

in the various concepts of planned reconstruction. But this would not affect the main issue.

Without entering into any detailed discussion of all their implications and contradictions, the principles for the establishment of a new economic order can be summarized as follows:

(1) Raising the standard of living through adjustment of wages and enlarged industrial and agrarian production;
(2) Prevention of mass unemployment;
(3) Free access of all countries to raw materials and natural resources and the elimination of all forms of discriminatory treatment in international commerce;
(4) Use of the scientific and economic apparatus, state control and organization, etc., which have proved so vital during the war, for future international planning. Among the institutions to be established after the war should be some form of price stabilization and control as well as joint allocation of markets and of production.
(5) Financing of government and other development schemes through international co-operation. The internal financing of reconstruction programmes undertaken by governments would be made possible by the maintenance of a high rate of taxation in peace-time as well.

Vigorous measures are thus planned for the countries of the West with a view to rectifying or alleviating the social and economic evils which have so gravely affected them, and there is no hesitation about profiting for this purpose from Russia's experience. Such projects and plans should be of even greater weight in the countries of the Middle East. Certain of the requisite conditions for intervention by the state or international bodies can be found here even more than in European countries. Economic organization is far less developed and complicated. Extensive measures to regulate economic life will therefore not be felt so keenly as they would be in the highly differentiated economic structures of Western countries. Years before the present war, some Middle Eastern countries entered the field of comprehensive planning in important economic spheres, preponderantly industry and transport. They understood that planning in Oriental countries means the use of state power for increasing production, whereas in Western countries planning was intended, as a rule, to restrict productive forces in order to avoid the consequences of plenty. Thus planning will find a partially paved way in Eastern countries after the war. In other respects, however, the application of such a policy will be more difficult; firstly, because a state-minded population prepared to co-operate fully in comprehensive schemes of economic and social reconstruction can scarcely be claimed to exist; and secondly, because the champions of the new reconstruction ideas in the West usually belong to the community on whose behalf they speak, whereas in Oriental countries hardly any voice hitherto raised in favour of the new concepts has come from the indigenous population itself. Planning depends for its success on the consent of the peoples concerned and their capacity for carrying it through. Here involved issues are at stake, which do not lend themselves to any rash conclusions as to the right kind of approach to the problems in question. One of the major problems arising in this context is the attitude of those at present controlling economic and political power. However, to do this subject justice a lengthy discussion of both the economic and political aspects would be required. We therefore content ourselves with pointing out that a mere change in the men occupying leading positions would not necessarily pave the way for reforms. The entire population has to be won over to the new programme, and trained for them. But governor and governed alike still need a large amount of education in this direction. The Oriental countries may therefore be regarded as occupying an intermediate position; they have neither reached the stage of highly developed capitalistic economies and the personal liberty and progress found in the West, nor have they advanced along the lines conducive to all-embracing collective planning of the kind practised in the Soviet Union. It would therefore mean a great deal for these countries, while undergoing a far-reaching and deep-seated transformation, to be spared both the disorganization resulting from unbridled economic activity based on private initiative and monopoly capitalism and such costly and cruel experiments as those tried in Russia in order to ascertain the most expedient method of establishing an economy planned or controlled on modern lines. To decide on the possibilities of development and the methods to be adopted in each case, it will be necessary to study conditions and their causes in the countries concerned. Without such close and as far as possible accurate knowledge of the facts, plans for development are doomed in advance. True, the difficulties encountered in the field of Oriental statistics are manifold and for certain specific problems still insurmountable.

Thus, for instance, one of the most significant groups of facts in modern planning, namely that referring to the composition and distribution of National Income, is known only to a very limited extent in Oriental areas. Hence other concepts had to be resorted to, although this sometimes involved the employment of coarser and more summary methods of computation and estimation than those applied in the well-explored countries of the West. For this reason alone an all-embracing and tight system of economic planning will prove impracticable in these parts of the world, whereas a policy of planned development, being a less rigid pattern, would definitely constitute an attainable goal.

In view of the great importance, in this context, of population increase in Oriental lands, we propose to deal first with the population trends and then with the standard of living and the level of income with a view to establishing a basis for development plans. At the same time, we shall be able to observe how far the social and economic features that have evolved in those countries are parallel to, or divergent from, those in Europe.

CHAPTER II

TRENDS OF POPULATION IN THE MIDDLE EAST

The population history of Oriental lands in the nineteenth century and down to the immediate present points to the existence there of certain trends that are no longer operative in other regions. This impression derives from tendencies observable not only in the Middle East itself but equally in the Mediterranean countries, beginning with Spain and Morocco and continuing deep into the territories of Southern Asia. It is true that figures illustrating the movements of population in the regions under consideration here, particularly during former periods, are remarkably scanty; nevertheless they provide a basis for conclusions which may facilitate the understanding of this biological phenomenon. In all cases where no preventive measures are applied or where the desire for reproduction and family increase was and still is effective, which in practice is true of many of the countries in question, a remarkably high reproductive rate is met with. The birth-rate *per mille* of the population is several times that of the countries of the temperate zones, with the sole exception of Russia. There, according to official figures, the fertility of the population is not lower than it is in Oriental and Mediterranean countries; even though family and group connections, together with the entire social structure, have been subject to tremendous changes since 1917.

The exceptionally high birth-rate, however, is balanced by a much higher mortality than can be found in northern countries. One is tempted to bear in mind the processes of the vegetable kingdom, and to compare the biological activity of the human beings of these zones with the unchecked vegetative growth of warm countries, where productive conditions are favoured by the climate and the decay is as considerable as the sequence of generations. Without further elucidating basic causes, the data assembled in the following table show the gap between the high birth- and death-rates of the Mediterranean and Oriental countries and the low figures of countries lying farther north. This can be particularly observed in the figures for surplus births (column 3 of the table on next page).[1]

[1] In view of the scarcity of data on the reproductive rate (gross and net) of the various Oriental countries, it was thought preferable to rely on crude birth and death rates.

Although the death-rate in the countries of Group A is considerably higher than in those of Group B, the total increase of population nevertheless by far exceeds that of Group B. A minimum of surplus births amounting to 9·7 in Group A can be compared with one of 0·8 in Group B.

The relation between birth- and death-rates tends to determine, by and large, the population problem arising in any given area where economic conditions remain static.[1] A rapid or

Group A.*	Births per 1,000.	Deaths per 1,000.	Surplus of Births per 1,000.
	(Average 1931–1935).†		
Bulgaria	29·3	15·5	13·8
Malta	33·2	22·1	11·1
Greece	29·5	16·5	13·0
Italy	23·8	14·1	9·7
Spain	27·0	16·3	10·7
Palestine	44·7‡	21·0	23·7 §
Egypt	42·9	27·4	15·5
Algeria ‖	33·1	17·1	16·0
Cyprus	29·8	14·8	15·0

Group B.*	Births per 1,000.	Deaths per 1,000.	Surplus of Births per 1,000.
	(Average 1931–1935).†		
England and Wales	15·0	12·0	3·0
Germany	16·6	11·2	5·4
France	16·5	15·7	0·8
Belgium	16·8	12·9	3·9
Denmark	17·7	10·9	6·8
Switzerland	16·4	11·8	4·6
Sweden	14·1	11·6	2·5
Norway	15·2	10·4	4·8

* Figures according to the *Statistical Yearbook of the League of Nations*.

† During the years 1936 to 1940 these figures have altered somewhat, partly because of measures touching on population policy. The changes, however, do not affect the conclusions reached here.

‡ Arabs: 50·2(!); Jews: 30·3.

§ Arabs: 24·9; Jews: 21·0.

‖ For 1934 only, excluding Europeans.

[1] There are, to be sure, certain factors which can modify these relations. Thus the climate and other natural conditions which permit a certain elasticity in the conditions of existence without any radical alteration in the structure of production, all play a part. The decisive factor, however, remains the relation between figures of births and deaths in all cases in which a certain degree of development of the population and resources has been reached and not exceeded.

even a slow but steady increase in population in a region where there is no way out for that increase is therefore liable to produce a population pressure which can easily lead to the phenomenon of over-population.

If the development of the Middle Eastern countries is considered from this viewpoint, the first impression is that the effect of the high birth-rate over several generations has been an enormous increase in population despite the mortality which is by no means negligible. The sole country for which reliable information is available for the period of the nineteenth century is Egypt. At the beginning of the nineteenth century the population of Egypt was estimated at about 2,490,000. Soon

GROWTH OF POPULATION SINCE 1800 *

	1800.		1900.		1938.		Growth in percentage 1900–38 (1900=100)
	Millions.	%.	Millions.	In percentage of 1800.	Millions.	In percentage of 1800.	
Europe	187	100	401	214·5	526	281·3	131·9
Africa	90	100	120	133·4	155	172·3	129·1
Asia	602	100	937	155·7	1,162	193·1	124·0
	Thousands.		Thousands.		Thousands.		
England and Wales	8,893	100	32,528	365·8	41,300	464·5	126·9
France	28,250	100	40,681	144·0	41,980	148·6	103·1
Germany	21,989	100	50,626	230·2	69,486	316·0	137·2
Egypt	2,460	100	9,734	395·7	16,415	667·3	168·6
Algeria	2,496†	100	4,739	189·9	7,184	287·9	151·5
Iraq	1,000	100	2,000	200·0	3,500	350·0	175·0
Syria	800	100	2,400	300·0	3,500	437·0	145·8
Anatolia	5,500	100	10,000	181·8	16,100	293·0	161·0
Palestine	300	100	600	200·0	1,500	500·0	250·0

* The absolute figures for non-Oriental countries and Egypt are taken from official sources (Statistical Yearbooks, etc.); the others are computations of the author.
† 1850.

after the middle of the century it amounted to 5,000,000. At the first modern census, held in 1897, the population was 9,715,000. In 1937 it amounted to 15,921,000 [1]; and meanwhile it has grown by a further 900,000. Hence the population here has multiplied in a fashion which can scarcely find its parallel anywhere else during the same period, even though the increase of population in other countries of the Old World during the

[1] 15,933,000 if nomads are included.

nineteenth century also reached considerable dimensions. Even more striking is the difference in the few decades of the twentieth century, during which Oriental populations have continued to increase rapidly, whereas many Western countries and the Continent as a whole are showing considerably reduced rates of increase.

GROWTH OF LARGE ORIENTAL TOWNS *

Jerusalem	1814 12,000	1880 35,000	1937 130,000
Haifa	1860 1,000	1880 5,000	1937 100,000
Tel-Aviv	—	—	1937 150,000
Beyrouth	1848 15,000	1880 80,000	1938 180,000
Aleppo	1845 77,000	1882 90,000	1938 272,000
Damascus	1849 150,000	1880 90,000	1938 261,000
Cairo	1848 254,000	1897 570,000	1937 1,312,000
Alexandria	1848 134,000	1897 320,000	1937 686,000
Ankara	1880 20,000	1927 75,000	1940 156,000
Istanbul	1900 1,125,000	1927 691,000	1940 789,000
Baghdad	1831 † 20,000	1900 145,000	1936 300,000
Izmir	1900 320,000	1927 154,000	1940 184,000

* In certain Oriental towns there has been a considerable contemporary decline in population, largely for political reasons. Istanbul and Izmir are instances. For the figures in the first two columns, descriptions and estimates from a great number of sources (official and non-official) have been cautiously employed; the data in the last column are mostly from recent censuses.

† Following an epidemic of plague.

For Oriental countries other than Egypt it is unfortunately necessary to depend on estimates. These nevertheless justify the assumption that increase of population, despite temporary setbacks due to epidemics, wars and the like, has been very considerable in these regions as well. An important index of this can be found in the growth of Oriental cities.

A comparison of the ratio between urban and total population in Oriental countries at various periods shows that here, too, developments analogous to those of Europe can be observed; although the quotas to be found for the growth of the cities in most Western countries have hitherto rarely been reached in the East. In the year 1800 only 3·6 millions or 3 per cent. of the urban population of Europe lived in towns with more than 100,000 inhabitants. Recent estimates show that in the industrialized countries of Europe the percentage has risen rapidly and uninterruptedly. In a number of countries from 33 per cent. to 50 per cent. of the population now live in towns with over 100,000 inhabitants.

In Oriental countries the percentage and growth of urban population is much slighter; but the movement of the figures during recent decades clearly shows that wherever factors similar to those operative in the West are at work, the same phenomena of increasing urbanization can be observed. Such factors are the socio-economic and political changes connected with industrialization, development of capital and administrative cities, etc.

SHARE OF LARGE-TOWN POPULATION IN TOTAL POPULATION

Country.	Year.	Total Population in 1,000s.	Thereof: in Towns with more than 100,000 inhabitants		Percentage of Large-Town Population for 1910.
			in 1,000s.	in %.	
England and Wales	1931	39,952	18,057	45·2	35·5
Australia	1933	6,630	3,152	47·5	37·3
Canada	1931	10,377	2,328	22·4	15·4
Denmark	1930	3,551	771	21·7	16·4
France	1936	41,907	8,824	21·1	14·5
Germany	1933	66,029	19,973	30·2	21·2
Netherlands	1930	7,936	2,162	27·2	23·3
Egypt	1937	15,921	2,123	13·3	9·2
Palestine	1935	1,308	265	20·1	—
Syria and Lebanon	1932	2,987	609	20·3	20·1
Turkey	1935	16,201	1,035	6·4	10
Iraq	1935	3,300	300	9·1	7·2

An illustration can be found in Cairo. At the Census of 1937 there was a population of 1,312,096 inhabitants, of whom only 812,069 were born in the town itself, while 433,160 came from Egyptian localities and 66,867 had immigrated from abroad. Other indications, such as registers of the number of persons liable to taxation in certain localities and districts in Oriental countries, show that in many cases the population during the nineteenth century was no more than a fraction of what it now is.[1]

The expectation of life in Oriental countries has improved again during recent years because the establishment of modern health institutions and the employment of modern methods for the prevention of epidemics, infant mortality, etc., are reducing the mortality figures.

Hence the following can be regarded as fundamental tendencies that have become manifest in the development of population in Oriental countries since the nineteenth century:

(1) The relative increase of population in most of these countries has in general been remarkably high, exceeding the relative growth of population of European countries, more particularly during the twentieth century.

(2) In the towns the increase of population is to a considerable degree due to internal migration. The influence of urban conditions of life, tending towards a reduction of the birth-rate, is compensated for by a decline in mortality thanks to improved health services.

(3) In Oriental countries as well urbanization manifests itself as an important phenomenon affecting population policy, and produces the same social problems as in the West, namely: depopulation of the poorer rural districts, unfavourable urban housing conditions creating slums and diseases, development of an uprooted working class lacking connections with family and village; and simultaneously new sources of livelihood in urban callings and a higher standard of living.

[1] For instance, Carl Ritter, *Vergl. Erdkunde der Sinai-Halbinsel usw.*, Berlin, 1852, p. 833, gives the number of tax-paying inhabitants of Palestinian towns in 1851 as follows: Jaffa, 3,072; Jenin, 800; Hebron, 4,071. The total population of the towns can be assessed by multiplying these figures by four. In this way he estimated that Jerusalem had a population of about 25,000.

CHAPTER III

POPULATION TRENDS AND NATIONAL INCOME

The constant increase in a population without any corresponding expansion in the scope of sustenance is described in accordance with current ideas as over-population. When the view first developed in Europe that there would be a permanent disharmony between growing population and available sources of livelihood, i.e. the average income per head, a school of population pessimists came into being who enunciated the now familiar unfavourable prognostications regarding the prospects of " surplus " populations. The nineteenth century proved that these theories were not generally valid. Despite an increase in population such as the world has probably never known, the prophesied pauperization did not ensue ; nor did the labouring masses in the towns become to an increasing degree the victims of poverty and starvation. On the contrary : despite all crises the increase in population was accompanied by a by no means inconsiderable rise in the total as well as the *per capita* national income.

England.		England.		U.S.A.		Germany.		Japan.	
Real Wages* (full work).		National Income produced per Head of Working Population.†							
1850	100	1860–69	100	1850	100	1854	100	1887	100
1900	183	1894–03	166	1900	199	1894–03	215	1908	137
1913	172	1913	185	1913	205	1913	244	1914	183
1937	221	1936	230	1936	246	1936	257	1936	468

* According to Layton and Crowther, *An Introduction to the Study of Prices*, 2nd edition, p. 274.

† Calculated on the basis of figures quoted by Colin Clark, *The Conditions of Economic Progress*, 1940, p. 148 (table).

At the same time the political importance of the workers has increased everywhere in a fashion scarcely imagined previously. Their influence on public opinion, parliaments and legislation, on economic policy and even on the direction of state policy itself, which they sometimes took into their own hands, has grown without interruption. Simultaneously, the relation between state and masses has changed fundamentally.

An annually increasing proportion of state income and public services is devoted to the section of the population with limited or no means. The reasons for this development need not be gone into here; the fact remains that the fears and warnings so frequently expressed at the beginning of the nineteenth century regarding the threat of overpopulation and pauperization have lost their weight.

What is the situation now in the countries of the Middle East? Many characteristics of general European cultural development cannot yet be observed here, or else are observable solely in their early stages; indeed it seems that one of these territories, namely Egypt, faces population problems strongly reminiscent of the descriptions of social conditions in the early days of industrial development in Europe. An unbroken increase of population within a few decades, which has led to the doubling of the population, is confronted by a natural limitation of the most important source of existence for the greater part of the population, namely the soil. The direct outcome is clearly a very low standard of living, with alarming health conditions among considerable sections of the population.

Is it inevitable, the question must be asked, that the Oriental countries with rising population must face developments by which the available means of existence grow steadily less per person? A study of conditions in other Asiatic countries where similar population conditions prevail does not lead to any immediate conclusion in this connection. Take the case of Japan. During the past sixty years the population of Japan has doubled without any increase in the territory available.[1] During the identical period, however, the standard of living of the population has become much higher. It has been calculated that during this time the average national *per capita* income has increased more than twofold, so that population and standard of living have risen simultaneously; a fact which at first sight seems somewhat surprising. Let us now turn to another Oriental country with a very notable increase of population, where an even more complex situation reigns as regards natural resources, viz. India. Although the standard of living of the Indian masses, judged even by Middle East levels, constitutes a minimum below which it would scarcely be possible to descend, nevertheless all reports on the conditions of life of the Indian population state that in the past these were even less favourable than they

[1] A. M. Carr-Saunders, *World Population*, 1936, p. 265.

are now. The Census Report of 1921 expresses itself as follows in this connection:

> The common people of Northern India were then (in the seventeenth century) undoubtedly almost naked. Blankets were unknown to them; shoes were seldom worn and little furniture was used, save a few earthen vessels. The population of the United Provinces is now 46 millions, and the people have long been more or less substantially clothed and shod; there are few who do not possess blankets, and brass pots are in almost universal use. . . . In recent times the standard of living has not risen in such an obvious way, but even during the last fifteen years (i.e pre-war period) there has been observable an increasing addiction to the use of small comforts and conveniences, such as tea, cigarettes, matches, lanterns, buttons, pocket knives, looking glasses—even gramophones—and of countless similar trifles. It seems unquestionable that up to the present time the number of the people and the standard of living have been rising together.

This quotation should not lead to any idealization of present conditions of life in India. A *per capita* national income of £4 is certainly far from permitting anything corresponding to our views of a decent standard of living. What affects the present issue is the following: An increase of the population in itself, even when territorial potentialities are restricted, is not of necessity accompanied by any deterioration of standards of life; on the contrary, it may be accompanied by a parallel improvement, or may even help to bring about such improvement, provided that certain prerequisites are fulfilled.

Hence the question arises as to the fashion in which such an improvement can come about. It is clear that any general improvement in the standard of living and the resultant rise in national income must be dependent upon conditions related in turn to the occupational structure of the forces participating in the economic process. The exhaustive researches of Colin Clark have served to prove that there exists a certain correlation between all these factors. A high *per capita* national income of the population always appears, together with an occupational structure in which a large percentage of the working population is engaged in manufacturing and intermediary services—the so-called secondary and tertiary callings. On the other hand, in countries where the overwhelming majority of the population is engaged in agriculture, i.e. " primary industries ", the average *per capita* national income is very low. The processing industries, including all industrial activities, mining and building, stand in the middle as " secondary industries ". Agricultural countries like India and China, but also Turkey, Iraq and Egypt, show a very low level of national income. In industrial countries this is multiplied, and reaches its maximum in the countries where a high average national income offers an opportunity for an increase in requirements which can be satisfied only by a great expansion of the so-called tertiary callings. Hence, for improving the living standard of a people, what is of importance is not only the raising of the general average income but also the distribution of this rise among the chief types of employment. A real improvement of the living standard of a nation presupposes a shift in the vocational structure in favour of the secondary and tertiary occupations which range high in the scale of income. Without these no rise in standard of living among the mass of the population is possible. Naturally the primary industries, i.e. agriculture and forestry, also provide opportunities for a rise in so far as they allow the use of improved methods and services. Where they assume an industrialized form (e.g. California and certain districts with artificial irrigation), they may even reach the income level of secondary callings. A glance at the following table shows that the *per capita* rise of income in the population tends to coincide to a very large degree with increasing industrialization. This is also confirmed by the conditions prevailing in the countries of the Middle East.

The establishment of a production structure favouring the increase of income is, however, as already mentioned, dependent on certain prerequisites without which any extension of the " living space ", that is the scope of economic progress, is impossible. What are these prerequisites? That there do exist

PURCHASING POWER OF AVERAGE INCOMES PER HEAD IN INTERNATIONAL UNITS *

(according to Colin Clark)

		Primary Production.	Secondary Production.	Tertiary Production.
Great Britain	1930	827	1,151	1,072
U.S.A.	1935	688	1,728	2,456
Germany	1928	440	810	935
Japan	1934	146	959	374
New Zealand	1935–6	1,872	1,653	1,296

* An International Unit equals the amount of goods and services which one dollar would purchase in the U.S.A. over the average of the period 1925–1934.

National Income per Head of Earning Population

	1936.	Primary.	Secondary.	Tertiary.
Palestine :				
Arabs . . .	—	LP. 27	83	95
Jews	—	LP. 60	127	134
Turkey * . . .	1935/36	LT. 131	407	852
Egypt † . . .	1922	LE. 55	120	80
Syria ‡ . . .	1936	£ 19	52	131

* Per head of earning males only.

† Calculated on data given by Dr. J. G. Levi in *L'Egypte Contemporaine*, 1922, p. 596. Figures in 1922 were inflated owing to the high price level.

‡ Estimates (excluding remittances from abroad), calculated in pounds sterling.

countries which have obviously reached saturation point as regards their increase in population is proved by the permanent emigration to be observed from such regions.

A simplified statement of the problem is : a country under population pressure that does not wish to export people must export goods. However, such goods must be suitable for sale ; and this in turn calls for the provision of raw materials, the manufacture, distribution and transport of which employs people. It may be a matter of the production of agricultural or industrial goods, but equally it may involve the exploitation of certain places in a country which attract tourists and induce them to expend large sums of money. Such services also belong to the category of export goods, as is indicated by the technical expression " invisible exports ". To-day, however, foreign markets are not regarded as the sole outlet for increased local production. A policy of raising the average internal purchasing power is being successfully pursued. Considerable increases in local production are apt to be marketed locally and will help to maintain a large population.

In both cases the necessary prerequisites do not differ in principle.

Hence the presence in a country of natural resources must be regarded as a primary condition ; although these are not always indispensable when complementary conditions are existent. The example of industrial Switzerland proves that raw materials do not have to exist in the country itself in order that an industry may be developed. Under certain conditions their importance diminishes as against that of specific qualifications of the inhabitants of a country, which suit them to achievements in modern industrial life. In addition, psychological qualities, particularly initiative, technical skill, a propensity for the processes of mechanical production and certain habits of consumption, may also be mentioned as decisive factors for the development of the natural resources of a country, i.e. for an increase of the volume of occupation. Finally, a not unimportant factor may be provided by certain external conditions, particularly external events such as, for instance, inventions and specific junctures of circumstances which can basically alter the existent economic opportunities from one day to the next. An obvious example can be found in the last and the present war, which particularly affected the countries of the Orient by giving a vast stimulus to industrialization. Similarly, the nationalism of youthful states has proved to be a driving force of great economic importance, the effect of which was not foreseen by anybody. Lastly, important transport developments, such as the cutting through of isthmuses which obstruct traffic or the conquest of transport by the motor-car, have become milestones in modern economic history through their stimulating effects.

If the countries of the Orient are now considered with these facts in mind, it will be found that the existent conditions favouring development can disperse all fears regarding any populatory saturation of these countries in the not-too-distant future. As regards the first condition of natural resources: the most important Oriental countries are marked by the joint effect of sun and water, which create agricultural possibilities of yield such as are unknown in more temperate zones. It is true that the density of population in Egypt is very high, and correspondingly the land available per family has been taken up to the utmost limit. On the other hand, however, countries like Iraq, Syria, Transjordan and Turkey are largely underpopulated and can, even on the most cautious estimates, provide many millions of people with opportunities of work and livelihood.

Although the agricultural potentialities of a country occupy pride of place in the Middle East, the other factors must in no way be underrated. Thus as regards mineral resources, the countries of the Middle East, though not to be compared with the particularly favoured regions of Europe or America, are by no means poor. The oil wells of Iraq, Iran, Egypt and Syria give these countries sources of extraordinary wealth apart from their direct value for industry and technology. Even the preliminary works prior to their opening gave a living to the thousands of people who built the plants. Once these are complete, they secure these countries a regular income at a level corresponding to a considerable part of the state budget.

However, other mineral products, such as the potash of the Dead Sea and the minerals of Turkey (coal, chromium, copper, etc.), are also important factors in determining the living-room available for the growth of population. Finally, the most important Oriental countries, from the Hellespont to the Nubian Desert, were ancient centres of culture in which a vast number of historical sites are found, frequently in beautiful landscapes ; so that there is a considerable opportunity for the further development of the tourist industry.

As regards the second condition, namely the human qualities on which the modern economic process is dependent, the Orient has in general not yet reached the level attained by Europe and America many decades ago for historical and sociological reasons. Only in Palestine has the immigration of Western elements introduced a class of qualified experts and professional workers fit for the direction of modern processes of production, who have called out such a degree of economic intensification on a comparatively small area as is unknown as yet in the other Oriental countries.

The third place was given to technical progress such as discoveries, inventions or international transport developments—factors from which the countries of the Middle East are already benefiting. A somewhat similar effect was produced by the growing tendencies towards economic nationalism in the world, which have enhanced the capacity of Oriental countries for absorbing the surplus population in industrial occupations. The number of persons engaged in industry and transport has risen without any falling off in the absolute figures for those engaged in agriculture.

As the factors described above come into play, the question of overpopulation assumes a different aspect. The most important teachings of modern population history, when applied to the countries of the Orient, would indicate that the population policy of these countries must include the rational utilization of cultivable and irrigable soil and an industrialization on a gradually expanding scale, which alters the ratio of primary (agriculture) to secondary and tertiary industries in favour of the two latter. Under no circumstances can conclusions as to absorptive capacity be based solely on the statistical relation between numbers of population and area of land available. It may even be said that the key to a regeneration of the Orient lies not in the conservation of its spaces, but on the contrary in their "reduction". The most fruitful economic and civilizing forces are called out not by distance but by proximity between men, by the effect of a dense population on the promotion of culture and progress.

Palestine, the population of which has doubled in less than twenty years, provides a striking example of the accuracy of this thesis. Naturally there were specific local factors at work which helped to make the potential resources of the country a reality. Such was the favourable disposition of the Jewish element for promoting development and the import of capital. Nevertheless the results are highly instructive. The standard of living, level of state expenditure, vital statistics, density of traffic, degree of productivity, and yield per land unit, all evince far more favourable indices in Palestine than in the neighbouring countries, despite the fact that the prognosis of twenty years ago was scarcely encouraging.

The table below aptly illustrates the different levels of economic development prevailing in the aforementioned countries :—

Country.	National Income *per Capita.**	State.		Length of Railway Lines per 10,000 Persons in 1938.	Number of Motor Vehicles Licensed per 1,000 Persons in 1938.	Import of Machinery and Apparatus *per Capita* in 1938.
		Revenue *per Capita* 1938–9.	Expenditure *per Capita* 1938–9.			
	£	£	£	km.		£
Egypt . . .	12	2·323	2·494	3·1	2·1	0·171
Palestine . .	26	3·958	3·870	5·3	6·2 ‡	0·619
Syria . . .	13	0·894 †	0·788 †	3·9	3·0	0·132
Iraq . . .	10	2·119	2·198	3·3	1·9	0·275
Turkey . .	19	3·286	2·958	4·2	0·6	0·218

* Figures for national income *per capita* refer mostly to 1936 or 1937. They are based on published investigations for Egypt, Turkey and Palestine, and are computed for Syria and Iraq.

† The low figure for Syria finds its explanation in the marked depreciation of the Syrian currency as against the pound sterling.

‡ If registered vehicles are taken into account, the above figure reaches 10.

For those familiar with the social and economic history of recent generations, the fact of the existence of the above-mentioned differences in development will not prove anything definite. Those who think in terms of longer periods will take into consideration all the experience offered by the industrial and agricultural development of Europe during the last century and of the resettlement of Palestine during the last generation; and they will not only regard the Oriental living-space as elastic and in no way saturated, but will, on the contrary, view it as a very important area for future settlement and development.

CHAPTER IV

MAJOR ECONOMIC AND SOCIAL PROBLEMS IN ORIENTAL COUNTRIES

The following common facts and trends have been established by us in respect of all Oriental countries :

(*a*) An extraordinary growth of population, which exceeds by far the rates of increase of most European countries.

(*b*) A progressive urbanization on a scale, however, which is still below that attained in Europe.

(*c*) A slow shifting in the occupational distribution of the population towards the secondary and tertiary occupations, the incomes of which greatly exceed those of the peasants (primary occupations).

(*d*) An exceedingly low average level of income in zones of predominantly agrarian structure.

Important as the establishment of these trends may be, our observations are not yet sufficient to enable us to conceive more detailed measures for future economic and social planning. Conditions and tendencies in the various countries under observation are not always identical. In one country the prevailing tendencies may bring about desirable results, whereas in others existent social evils may be aggravated by them. Hence what is required is a further elucidation of the basic facts, particularly as regards the economic structure and the ratio between production and consumption, before more concrete conclusions can be reached as to the development capacity of the countries in question and the suitability of programmes for such development.

1. Egypt

We shall deal with Egypt first. It heads all Oriental countries in density of population, but for the same reason it has to face difficulties which do not exist or exist only partially in the remaining territories.

The *total area* of Egypt, including desert regions, figures at approximately 1,000,000 sq. kms. Of this area, however, only about $3\frac{1}{2}$ per cent. or 35,000 sq. kms. is, or can be, cultivated ; the remaining portion being desert land and unpopulated except for a scanty number of Bedouins. Two-thirds of the area capable of cultivation lie in the Delta. In this district nearly half the Egyptian population live and here most of the more advanced towns are situated including, in the north-west and north-east, the two great ports of Alexandria and Port Said; which are so important for Egypt's traffic with countries abroad.

From the following table it is plain that in the course of fifty-five years an excessive increase of population has occurred. Besides the expansion of the urban areas (Governorates), a very notable increase took place in the rural districts which form the bulk of the area of Lower and Upper Egypt.

AREA, POPULATION AND DENSITY PER SQ. KM. BY DISTRICTS (CENSUSES 1882–1937)

	Governorates (Cairo, Alexandria and Suez Canal Zone).	Upper Egypt.	Lower Egypt.	All Egypt.*
Area in sq. kms. (1937) . . .	392	12,047	21,745	34,184
Population (in 1,000s)				
1882 . . .	697	2,693	3,279	6,805
1897 . . .	1,004	3,932	4,655	9,715
1907 . . .	1,141	4,577	5,417	11,287
1917 . . .	1,389	5,187	6,095	12,751
1927 . . .	1,843	5,710	6,531	14,218
1937 . . .	2,249	6,423	7,139	15,933
Density per sq. km.				
1882 . . .	1,778	223	151	199
1897 . . .	2,561	326	214	284
1907 . . .	2,910	380	249	330
1917 . . .	3,543	431	280	373
1927 . . .	4,701	474	300	416
1937 . . .	5,737	533	328	466

* Inhabited area, excluding the area of frontier districts and lakes. The total area of Egypt, all desert areas included, is roughly 994,000 sq. kms. Population figures in this column include Arab nomads and others in respect of frontier districts not specified in the tables. In 1937 their number was 122,000; thereof 12,000 nomads.

Figures of population density in Egypt count among the highest of the kind known in the world at present. This density, which has increased during recent decades, is not the outcome of very intensive industrial activity fostered by rich natural resources and mining deposits such as favour a high density in the strongly industrialized mining areas of Europe and the U.S.A. ; on the contrary, this increase has been going on without any corresponding expansion of the living space, and has led to an exceedingly low standard of living and a reduction of the *per capita* share of the population in the boons which the fertile land of Egypt provides.

GROWTH OF CROP AREA AND TOTAL POPULATION

	1886	1927	1937	1962 *
Total Crop Area in Feddans . . .	6,670,000	8,661,250	8,358,284	13,000,000
Percentage Increase over 1886.		29·8	25·3	95
Total Population	8,045,000	14,177,864	15,920,000	24,000,000
Percentage Increase over 1886 .		76·2	97·9	198·3
Persons per 100 Feddans of Crop Area	120	164	190	185

* Estimate for 1962 : figures for the other years are taken from Cleland.

This table shows that the increase in men was far higher than the increase in crop area. Between the years 1886 and 1937 the population rose by 97·9 per cent, whereas the crop area increased only by 25·3 per cent. On an average there lived in 1937 190 men on 100 Feddans as against 120 in 1886. A similar result is obtained per head during the period 1885 to 1935 at intervals of decades. Here, too, we find a depressing reduction in the extent of the *per capita* area from 0·83 to 0·53 Feddans. During the same time the area under cotton, which constitutes the principal cash crop, rose from 1,326,000 to 1,732,000 Feddans.

Year.	Population (in 1,000s).	Crop Area in Feddans (1,000s).	Area per Head.	
			in Feddans.	in %.
1886 . . .	8,045	6,670	0·83	100
1895 . . .	9,285	6,552	0·71	86
1905 . . .	10,958	7,481	0·68	82
1915 . . .	12,443	7,619	0·61	74
1925 . . .	13,932	8,457	0·61	74
1935 . . .	15,373	8,101	0·53	64

To explain this development, it will be necessary to give a more detailed description of economic conditions, and to add some data on the social and health conditions of the greater part of the Egyptian population.

Economic Conditions: Agriculture

Agrarian conditions in Egypt are to a large extent reflected in the Fellahin's economic and social position. Up to the present day the most significant feature of Fellahin economy is a standard of living which is singularly low as compared with Western concepts. The changes of millennia have, for all the marks left in Fellahin economy, scarcely brought about any alteration in this extraordinary absence of needs, or at least in the readiness to undergo privation. Expenditure on clothing, housing, furniture and even food requirements can hardly ever have been more scanty or monotonous than they are to-day, after a period of unusual prosperity in the first years following the last war, which benefited even the Fellahin to a certain degree. The traveller who, cherishing conceptions of Egypt's proverbial wealth and the Delta's inexhaustible fertility, visits Egyptian villages for the first time will be sorely disappointed at the material standard he encounters. Now as ever the majority of Egyptian villages are built of dried Nile sludge. The interior of the houses is indescribably primitive. There is hardly any furniture, its place being taken by dried reeds, which serve the function of beds as a substitute for straw mats. The item of clothing in a Fellah's budget is of minor importance. Clothing expenses for children are next to nothing, and even with the Fellah himself and his wife purchases are so rare that they remain completely in the background if compared with the remaining items of expenditure.

In these circumstances, the pressure of an ever-increasing population in Egypt has only two possibilities of alleviation: it may for once find an outlet in a strong migration from the country into the towns, or else may lead to a marked reduction in natural increase. As neither of these cases has occurred to any considerable extent, we find a steady partition and splitting up of the Fellahin's landed property and, consequently, a land scarcity such as has hardly been experienced anywhere else.

There has, it is true, also been a tendency towards urbanization. Egypt's urban population shows a larger increase in number, though not solely on account of migration, than that of the rural districts. Above all, the absorptive capacity of the larger cities has proved to be fairly considerable. In 1937, the five principal urban areas alone contained 14 per cent. of the total population. Taking the smaller urban centres into account as well, it is found that the percentage rose from 14·3 in 1897 to 18·5 in 1937.

THE URBANIZATION OF EGYPT FROM 1897 TO 1937

	1897.	1907.	1917.	1927.	1937.
	Population Figures in Thousands.				
The five Governorates: (Urban Areas of Cairo, Alexandria, Canal Zone, Suez, Damietta):					
In absolute figures	1,004	1,141	1,389	1,843	2,249
In percentage of total population	10·3	10·2	10·9	13·0	14·1
Additional 14 Urban Areas (District Towns):					
In absolute figures	392	409	495	605	695
In percentage of total population	4·0	3·7	3·9	4·3	4·4
Degree of Urbanization . . .	14·3	13·9	14·8	17·3	18·5

Much more conspicuous, however, and far more important as regards the peasant's level of subsistence was the second tendency of incessant breaking up of landed property into small and even tiny allotments. This process of decomposition, which has gone on without a break for many decades down to the present day, does indeed constitute a particularly characteristic feature of Egyptian agriculture. In the course of less than forty years this development has brought about almost a quadruplication in the number of smallholders (owning up to 5 Feddans), as contrasted with the remaining categories of landowners in which there has hardly been any appreciable alteration.

Apart from the excessive parcellation of the cultivated land, causing the plots of countless farmers to be reduced below the subsistence level, there are the tenants who are burdened with exorbitant rents. It sounds almost incredible that a wretched farmer should be called upon to pay a rent of between £E.6 and £E.22 for a plot measuring 1 Feddan (= 4,200 sq. metres), when under exceptionally favourable circumstances (excellent crop, high prices) he can at best eke out a meagre livelihood.

Under ordinary conditions, his is a desperate struggle for existence, to say nothing of bad years. A tale like the following, which represents a typical case, may serve to illustrate this point :

DISTRIBUTION OF LAND-OWNERSHIP IN EGYPT, 1896–1939

Land Owned according to Size Groups in Feddans.	Number of Proprietors.*					
	1896.	1906.	1916.	1926.	1936.	1930.
Up to 1 .	—	—	1,006,866	1,391,533	1,677,536	1,751,587
1– 5 .	611,074†	1,084,001†	473,688	531,324	564,700	571,133
5–10 .	80,810	76,935	76,641	81,597	84,617	84,609
10–20 .	41,276	36,951	36,982	39,027	39,643	40,494
20–50 .	22,225	20,029	19,852	21,638	21,799	21,179
Over 50 .	11,875	12,665	12,297	12,465	12,420	12,248
Total	767,260	1,230,581	1,626,326	2,077,584	2,400,715	2,481,250

* According to an explanation received by the author, an owner of several parcels of land appears several times as proprietor in the statistics in question, if his parcels are situated in different fiscal administrative units.

† Including estates of 1 Feddan and less.

A Fellah, whose gamus (= buffalo) was seized to cover his debt, described his position to the inquirer as follows :

" I have taken two Feddans on lease, each for £E.12, and have expended £E.5 on manure, seeds, etc., in respect of each of them, to say nothing of my labour, that of my children and the help of my animals during the whole year. And here is the result : one Feddan has yielded 4 kantars of cotton, sold at £E.12 ; the other—5 ardebs of grain and 7 of maize, sold at £E.13. My income being £E.25 of which £E.10 have already been spent, what else can I do to pay off my rent but to sell my buffalo ? "

" But since you are losing, why do you go on renting the plot ? "

" Because farming is the vocation I have inherited from my forefathers, and I can do no other work."

" Then why do you pay such a high price for the land ? "

" Because landowners in this region have united to maintain the price of the land, and the Fellahin do not know how to make it go down." [1]

There have been several attempts to lower the exorbitant rent payable to landowners. The Egyptian Government has decreed that farm rents be reduced by between 25 and 40 per cent. for the years 1929, 1930, 1931 and 1932, but such reductions were made only when the position of the tenant was so desperate as to leave no alternative. If intervention by Government was possible in years of distress, it should also prove feasible in

[1] From the daily *Al Ahram* of 3rd November, 1936, quoted (in French) by H. Habib Ayroub, Fellahs, 1942, pp. 67–8.

normal times. It would go a long way towards relieving the position of tenants, and a progressive Government should not hesitate to embark upon such a policy even in the face of opposing landowners. Until now no Government, when asked to intervene in favour of the tenants, has dared to touch the vested interests of landowners by measures having a permanent effect.

To the problems connected with tenure relations another difficulty must be added. In Egypt, economic life depends on the world market more than in any other country of the Middle East. The share of cotton and its by-products, which are the principal sources of cash income, in Egyptian agriculture, is so considerable that every fluctuation in the values of these products immediately affects the entire economic life of the country. The fixing of cotton prices, however, is almost completely beyond the range of any possible Egyptian influence ; prices on cotton markets in Egypt closely follow the lead of English and American prices respectively as a result of which the whole country, including even the remotest Fellahin village, always shows prompt reactions to international fluctuations. In 1935 the proportion of cotton and cotton-seed in the total export of Egypt amounted to 80 per cent., in 1936 to 82 per cent., and in 1937 to 84 per cent. In addition, other important agricultural products such as onions, rice, eggs and sugar have to a large extent become export articles, which leads to a considerable dependence on the world market in these agricultural branches as well.

Living Standard and Health Conditions

What are the conditions under which the rural population of Egypt, who form the bulk of the inhabitants of that country, eke out their livelihood ? Revenue figures of agriculture alone point to an exceedingly low level of subsistence. An annual income of from £20 to £30 for a family of between 5 and 6 persons constitutes the usual peace-time standard ; this is a *per capita* income which, whether earned in kind or in specie, scarcely suffices to cover the barest necessities of life.

Matters are far worse in the case of agricultural workers, who possess no land of their own or at best only a tiny plot. These depend for their existence on the scanty wages of 2 to 3 piastres a day which they earn during a working season of about 6 to 8 months. Their annual income thus averages from 5 to 6 pounds only, and the accounts describing the appalling state of health of the rural population are therefore not at all surprising.[1] The Report of the Finance Commission of the Senate for the year 1940–1 states, *inter alia*, that about 250,000 children die annually under the age of five. The infant mortality rate, according to official figures, is 193 per 1,000 as against,

COST OF LIVING OF A FAMILY OF FIVE IN THREE DIFFERENT PARTS OF EGYPT—1931 [2]

	Lower Egypt.	Middle Egypt.	Upper Egypt.
	£E.	£E.	£E.
Food, Fuel and Equipment:			
Maize and some barley, 33 to 39 bus.	5·760	4·800	6·300
Wheat, 3 to 5 bus.	1·500	0·600	1·700
Fenugreek, to mix with maize, 1 or 2 bus.	0·450	0·400	—
Meat, 96 lb.	2·400	2·400	2·400
Butter, 12 to 32 lb., and oil, 6 qts.	1·440	1·200	0·960
Cheese, 120 to 200 lb.	1·800	1·000	0·400
Vegetables, 135 to 275 lb.	0·240	1·170	1·450
Rice, 220 lb.	1·020	—	—
Fruits, sugar-cane, dates, melons, etc.	1·000	1·000	0·750
Salt, 66 lb.	0·150	0·120	0·150
Sugar, 100 to 140 lb., coffee, tea, 5 to 11 lb.	2·040	1·980	0·700
Soap, 30 lb.	0·420	0·420	0·420
Petroleum for lighting, 15 to 20 galls.	0·240	0·320	0·320
Utensils, pots, dishes, mats	0·100	0·100	0·200
Haircutting and shaving	0·300	0·300	0·300
Tobacco	3·600	3·600	3·600
Bedding, blankets, etc.	1·000	1·000	1·250
Sub-total	23·460	20·410	20·900
Clothing, Husband	1·090	1·250	2·100
Clothing, Wife	0·790	1·250	1·700
Clothing, Children	0·990	0·420	1·240
Grand Total	26·330	23·330	25·940

for example, 140 in Palestine (Arab population) and 116 in Cyprus. The general death-rate in Egypt at the beginning of the twentieth century, 25·3 per 1,000, had gone up to 27·2 in 1937, notwithstanding the fact that all other countries showed a simultaneous decline in their mortality figure. Even in India

[1] The following impressive description of existing conditions was given by Aly Shamsy Pasha, a noted Egyptian economist and politician: "... les ouvriers agricoles reçoivent chacun d'eux un salaire quotidien d'à peine supérieur à P.T.1.—La conscription militaire a mis en lumière la véritable faiblesse physique dont souffre cette classe de la population par suite de la sousalimentation et des maladies qui en découlent ... de 2,440,000 propriétaires fonciers que compte le pays, 2,282,000 ne possèdent en tout que 1,879,000 Feddans sur une totalité de 5,334,000 Feddans, alors que seulement 12,450 propriétaires fonciers possèdent plus de 2,250,000 Feddans." (Cf. *L'Informateur Financier & Commerciel* of 12 December, 1941.)

[2] Cleland, *The Population Problem in Egpyt*, 1936, p. 119.

the death-rate recorded did not exceed 22 to 23 per 1,000, to say nothing of the figures for European countries which are considerably below those for Egypt. An aggravating feature in this connection is the inordinately large incidence of serious disease: 90 per cent. of the Egyptian population suffer from trachoma (ophthalmia granulosa), 75 per cent. from bilharzia, 50 per cent. from ankylostoma, 50 per cent. from worm diseases. The number of people afflicted with tuberculosis exceeds 300,000. To these must be added the very numerous diseases which are not due to the specific conditions of Egyptian agriculture (permanent irrigation) or climate. Cleland, whose statements are based on the findings of medical authorities, describes the position as follows:

> Enough has been said here to give a hint as to the reason for the tolerance of the Fellaheen towards their miserable condition. In short it is this: The vast majority have worm diseases which enervate their bodies and dull their minds and diminish their ambitions to a sufficient extent, so that they have no courage to face an adventure into some unknown area where they might improve their condition. They are fearful lest any poor, dry crust which they do have, may escape them. While the high death-rate in Egypt is undoubtedly due in part to the low vitality of the population as a result of bilharziasis and ankylostoma, yet it is apparent that the peculiar effect of these diseases is not to reduce numbers so much as to increase numbers. Such diseases of slow death have the unfortunate result of filling up space with large numbers of persons living more or less below par, and incapable of employing normal human energy for bare self-maintenance, or for adding in any degree to the nation's social inheritance, or for bestirring themselves adequately either within or away from their impoverished, crowded quarters. Add to this situation the constant trouble with eyes, frequently accompanied by severe pain, a constant baffle to all activities, and who can say that the people's mental vision would not be as confused and dim as their physical vision?[1]

A population whose vitality has been ruinously affected by enervating diseases and who are, moreover, deprived of all means necessary to ease their position or to take any precautions, are bound to become indifferent to any suggestion or expedient calculated to improve their lot. Factory inspectors report, for instance, that, in accordance with regulations, sanitary facilities, buildings, dining-halls, etc., are frequently provided by industrial enterprises for the benefit of their workmen, but that almost

[1] Cleland, op. cit., p. 87.

all of these conveniences turn out to be superfluous, since the majority of the workers are making no use of them. Similarly we are told that power stations and water-works are found in a large number of villages, but the inhabitants for the most part refuse the electric light offered to them and go on using the petrol lamp, and they prefer the water from the canal near the village to the drinking water supplied to them by the local water station. And this despite the fact that the danger involved in such practices has been pointed out again and again to the Fellahin.

The Egyptians have recognized the dangers involved in a far-reaching lack of education for the development of the Egyptian people; they are also aware of the inadequacy of the existent school system, which is devoted to the combating of illiteracy. Article 19 of the Egyptian Constitution provides for free school attendance, which is obligatory for both male and female juveniles between the ages of 7 and 12 years. Punishment of the parents is prescribed if they do not send their children to school; provided that the school lies within two kilometres of the village. Though many years have passed since this Article was incorporated in the Constitution, it has remained on paper. The number of pupils enjoying education has, it is true, increased considerably, but the percentage of illiteracy remains shockingly high.

The resistance to the general extension of compulsory school attendance derives not only from village parents who are not willing to do without the assistance of their children, but is also supported by classes who regard the spreading of education as possibly leading to the development of an intellectual proletariat.

In this form the problem affects not only Egypt but also other Oriental countries. Which direction should an educational policy adapted to the special conditions of Oriental countries follow? The subject has for years been occupying the minds of the governments concerned and their advisers.

In actual fact elementary schools have been established in large numbers during recent years. The reports on the state of these schools, however, are anything but encouraging. Statements by the Chief Medical Officer regarding the hygienic and social conditions in rural schools show that a vast amount still remains to be done before anything comparable with the standards of Western countries is reached:

> It is to be regretted that teachers pay no attention to health education and are satisfied to indoctrinate their pupils by requiring

them to memorize " empty " meaningless phrases, without seeing to it that the children actually apply them. Very often we observed on pupils' faces swarms of flies covered with dirt, while the teacher was giving them a lesson on the danger of flies and dirt, without taking pains to ask them to drive away the flies or clean the dirt. Remarking on this point to the teacher, I was told by the latter that inspectors had warned them against strictness in cleanliness, lest the children should deviate from their environment. As far as I know, dirt is never the necessary accompaniment of any environment.

Similarly, the physicians who visit these schools advise the children never to neglect wearing their shoes, but their advice is futile because the teachers do not follow it up, although wearing shoes is the best preventive measure against some of the parasitic diseases.[1]

One should not lend oneself to easy generalizations of these and similar observations. But it is difficult to escape the impression that there is still a formidable task to be fulfilled, in view of the appalling degree of illiteracy which comprises about 80 to 90 per cent. of the Egyptian masses.

Industrial Development

The vast predominance of the agricultural sector in Egyptian economy makes it obvious that only a limited place is at present occupied by industry in this country. At the same time it should be appreciated that there has been industrial development in Egypt for decades, with remarkable results in various economic branches, particularly since the last war. The present war has increased these tendencies towards industrialization still more.

According to the 1937 Census 393,563 males and 44,439 females, in all 438,002 persons, were engaged in industry and handicrafts. In addition, a further 10,800 persons were employed in extractive industries.[2] Unfortunately the estimates of the Finance Commission of the Senate in connection with the Budget of 1941–2 are based on other methods of computation, so that it is impossible to make a comparison of developments during the past five years.

From another source, the " Egyptian Federation of Industries ", it emerges that a census covering half of Egypt's industrial undertakings gives a wages and salaries total of £E.5,213,000 for 129,400 employees or about £E.40·3 as wages or salary *per capita*.

[1] From a report by the Chief Medical Officer of the Ministry of Education submitted to the Minister of Education in 1932. (Vide A. Boktor, *School and Society in the Valley of the Nile*, 1936, p. 193.)

[2] Doubtless certain of these figures apply to persons who are engaged not in industrial undertakings proper but in workshops.

As this sum also includes salaries that are far larger, it may be assumed that an average monthly wage of £E.3 is not exceeded.

Important as the fact of a higher wage per head of those engaged in industry may be in itself when compared with the minimal earnings of agricultural workers, it can have no decisive effect on the present living conditions of Egypt's population as a whole in view of the restricted scope of the country's industry to-day. The number of those engaged in industry in 1941 does not appear to have exceeded 10 per cent. of all those gainfully employed. Even disregarding this, however, a wage of 10 piastres a day for a town-dweller is a sum which permits only the barest minimum of existence, more particularly if he has to maintain dependants.

2. Iraq

A number of features in the social and economic structure of Iraq closely resemble those of Egypt, especially as regards the standard of living of the peasantry, the importance attached there to river irrigation, and the predominance of agricultural occupations. Yet this should not delude us into ignoring the fundamental difference in the development potentialities of the two countries. Even large amounts of capital investment and huge technical improvements would not change the fundamental fact of a state of excessive density in Egyptian agriculture within its present boundaries. In Iraq it is just the reverse. The cultivable area of the latter country is largely untilled. In contrast to the overcrowding of the Egyptian land, it is the under-development of Iraq's agriculture, caused by lack of people, which accounts for the miserable conditions of life prevailing among the rural population. Statesmen and judges of the country's agriculture have always stressed that what Iraq most required was people. However, in studying the agrarian conditions of Iraq, we are aided to a lesser degree than in the case of other Oriental countries by accurate figures, as data of this kind are very scantily provided in that land. Iraqi population statistics in particular are not very lucidly arranged, and it is difficult to ascertain any precise figure since a modern population census based on scientific methods has never been taken. Moreover, the absence of any comprehensive land surveys and registers presents an obstacle to any exact calculation of the relation between area and population in the different zones, i.e. the relative density of the agricultural population.

District Authorities in various parts of the country are in possession of certain figures, but, like all other data referring to land conditions, these should be used only with considerable reservations.

Notwithstanding all this, the facts mentioned below allow for certain conclusions to be made.

In no other Middle East country outside Egypt (which, as already stated, shows a certain similarity in natural features) is soil of such potential fruitfulness to be found as in Iraq with its rich silt land between the two rivers. The Tigris and the Euphrates have for centuries carried enormous quantities of silt from the north-west to the south-east, thus creating one of the most fertile regions in the world. Under prevailing conditions irrigation is a vital need in Iraq as it is in Egypt. Properly irrigated as it used to be in the days of antiquity and the early Middle Ages, Iraq might again become one of the world's foremost granaries. Where irrigation is neglected, the landscape in Iraq presents a picture of arid steppe land.

Owing to its natural fertility and the relative simplicity of the irrigation problem (as far as the procuring of water is concerned), Iraq offers possibilities for agricultural development such as are seldom found elsewhere. To-day they are mostly disregarded. For reasons of climate it is practically out of the question for people from Europe to engage in agriculture in Iraq, to say nothing of the social and political problems involved in such settlement. Nevertheless it is quite conceivable that a none-too-remote future may witness settlement activities on a far larger scale than is at present found in Iraq, both as regards inland colonization, i.e. settlement of the Bedouins on the soil, and the influx of Arab peoples from more densely populated Oriental countries.

Iraq's agricultural development is considerably influenced by the social structure of its population, which shows a variety of rural types ranging from the purely nomadic tribesmen, preserving intact the tradition of past centuries, to the suburban market gardener, running an electrically-driven irrigation plant. Distinct groups are formed by the mountaineers of the north and north-east, and by the semi-nomadic tribes on the banks and marshes of the two rivers and along the canal system. In the mountain villages, the prevailing land property conditions are similar to those of other parts of the Middle East. Land is owned by a few rich landowners, who employ the village population as labourers and shepherds on the usual share system, so that only 30 to 40 per cent. of the yield is left to the actual cultivator. In addition to the share they draw from the owner's crop, the peasants and their families sometimes supplement their meagre yields by keeping a few sheep or by cultivating some insignificant plot left to them, and by the occasional sale of fuel to the towns. The standards of living are often very much lower than in the neighbouring countries, which are in closer contact with westernizing influences.

The income of the Iraqi Fellah is extremely low since he must share his meagre harvest among many. Not only does the landowner or the tenant to whom he is a sub-tenant take a lion's share of his yield, but he has further to make contributions to the State and to numerous people, partly self-installed, partly representatives of authorities and of landowners. In addition to the Government Tax he has to meet the claims of the Serkal, the Wahash, and others mediating between him and the aforementioned claimants. The share the Fellah ultimately retains for himself and his family, expressed in money terms, works out at £6 to £10 annually in the Northern District, and about one and a half to twice these amounts in the Central and Southern Districts, according to pre-war prices. Even when compared with the low incomes derived by Fellahin in the neighbouring countries, these figures are surprisingly small. It is obvious that under these conditions, standards of life cannot be other than extremely primitive. This backwardness may be seen externally from the appearance of the Fellah's farm, his house (in large parts of the country nothing more than a reed hut), and his equipment not costing more than a few pounds.

The tribal cultivators in the river basins are a rural type of importance and their social structure continues to exhibit feudal features. The leading position of the sheikh is, however, conditioned not only by hereditary rights but also by definite rights or titles on the tribal lands or crops. Originally the communal ideas of property and the equality of crop shares among all members of the tribal brotherhood were dominant characteristics of their tribal life. But more recent development has brought with it, in accordance with a more individualistic outlook, the increased material dominance of the sheikh, who holds the best part of the land and is acquiring a position not dissimilar from that of the large property-owner elsewhere. In addition to being the hereditary chief, he is now the master for whom the other members of the tribe must work, losing their former free independent right in the tribal community.

In Iraq perhaps more than in other countries of the Middle East, tribal settlement is an urgent and important question. To the usual aims of agrarian reform there is added the necessity of transforming the nomadic tribes into settled cultivators. This is one of the most complicated and interesting problems which agrarian reform in the East has to face. As semi- and entirely nomadic tribes form such an important part of the population, this question is of particular magnitude. There are two main aspects to be considered : on the one hand, the protection of the already settled population against the raids and land claims of the Bedouin tribes, and on the other, the transformation of nomads into settled cultivators, and the consolidation of their social and economic life.

Rural reform, however, is faced by other more serious difficulties caused by both the type of farming practised and the chaotic state of land rights. Without at least a partial solution of these problems no progress is possible. It is a practice for the Iraqi peasant in many parts of the country to move from area to area as the fertility of each successive piece of land is exhausted. Manuring is not practised, nor is attention paid to the restitution of soil properties. Owing to this mobility the peasant does not pay particular attention to any one plot of land and is not interested in improving and intensifying his farming, for which he also lacks the necessary resources and knowledge. This type of mobile agriculture, dating from remotest antiquity and rooted in tradition, is possible only in a country where there is a big surplus of land and land ownership is unregulated ; an almost anarchical state of land rights is the logical consequence of such a practice.

It is scarcely an exaggeration to say that under such circumstances not much has been achieved in the field of individual farming. Neither has a far-sighted reform of land tenure been carried out, as suggested by Sir Ernest Dowson, one of the most penetrating students of Iraq's land questions. The tribal areas have remained nearly untouched by land settlement activities, and the significant remark made by Sir Ernest has lost nothing of its actuality : " So long as tribal and other communal divisions remain strong, unrestricted individual freedom to dispose of land would be dangerous to public peace and contentment." Freedom to deal with the land according to the necessity which the best possible use requires is, however, a pre-condition of all progress. If this right is absent, the small peasant and tenant remains a chattel in the hands of the landed proprietor. The big landowners, whether of recent date or descendants of the old landed aristocracy, are thus the real masters of the country and decide the living conditions of the peasant class and the rural workers. But it appears impossible to preserve for long a social order based on conditions pertaining to a past age and on isolation from the outside world, when fresh contacts with the West, a virtually unlimited scope for agricultural expansion, new transport developments and the rise of a modern State provide a constant stimulus to social and economic advance.

Industrialization

A few words may be added here on the industrial position of Iraq. Iraq is a predominantly agrarian country and its industrial production is still in its infancy. The few undertakings worthy of the name "industrial" owe their existence partly to state support which, by the way, is given in a less active and systematic form than in other Middle East countries such as Turkey and Iran. A number of bills were enacted with a view to stimulating the establishment of industrial enterprises by providing for certain preferential customs tariffs and exemption from taxes; the Government has further allocated amounts for industrial credits and is administrating them through a newly established Agricultural and Industrial Bank. In one respect, however, Iraq very widely enjoys the fruits of industrial achievements, even though the latter represent a sector *per se* within the country's economy. The oil industry is by far the most important industrial branch in the country, and although run by foreign concessionnaires, it has contributed its share to progress. Yet despite all this, the whole industrial sector has remained extremely small, and the number of those employed in modern industry hardly exceeds one-half per cent. of the total earners.

3. Other Oriental Countries

No detailed analysis of economic conditions in other Oriental countries is possible within the framework of this book. Yet many of the foregoing general remarks as to the standard of living of the peasant class apply, *mutatis mutandis*, to other Oriental regions as well. A short description summarizing their peculiar features may, however, be added. Any traveller or visitor touring Middle Eastern countries must be deeply impressed by the singularly low housing standard of rural areas. Villages of mud and earth in the interior of the Anatolian steppes, in the river valleys and large plains of Syria, the stone huts and hovels in the mountains of Palestine, Syria and Cyprus mostly show an almost incredibly low level of housing comfort, equipment and hygiene. True, the houses are sometimes ingeniously adapted to the physical conditions of their environs from the point of view of material used, expenditure involved in erection and form of the dwellings themselves. But many features affecting health, such as the absence of ventilation, the lack of equipment, even light furniture and conveniences, the crowding of men and animals under the same roof, the muddy and dusty courtyards, etc., are clearly grave defects, the negative outcome of which can scarcely be over-estimated. Even if housing conditions in certain well-to-do villages have improved or are improving, the fact remains that the majority of the rural populations concerned are housed in a manner rightly regarded as below the acknowledged minimum level.

It should not be difficult to arrive at similar conclusions as to the state of nutrition among the peasant population. It is true that quantitatively speaking the Fellah is able to meet his food requirements ; he does it mostly by a large consumption of hydrates (starch) and vegetables. But his needs for the more expensive foodstuffs, which contain the important animal proteins and vitamins, are only partially satisfied, and from the viewpoint of modern nutrition there are grave deficiencies in this diet. If, according to modern nutrition theory, the diet even of fully developed Western countries needs to be improved decisively, how much more can this be claimed in the case of the Oriental populations, with their exceedingly low income level.

This level of income is, of course, the outcome of a combination of factors, economic, social and political, one of them being the system of land tenure which has been prevalent in the Middle East for centuries. Although statistics on distribution and size of holdings are exceedingly scarce, except for Egypt, a very considerable proportion, in some regions more than half, of Oriental peasants cultivate their land under the share system. The land belongs to the land proprietor, whereas the tenant tills the plot assigned to him by a traditional lease arrangement. The holdings are very small in irrigated areas where the amount of labour needed is high and the family's working capacity is taxed to the utmost, while the average size tends to increase with the need for extensive farming. The most conspicuous feature of the share system is the low share apportioned to the tenant. It may differ slightly from region to region and is modified by local usage—whether, for instance, animals, implements, equipment or seed are provided by the landowner or not. But the rule is that the tenant seldom keeps more than a third to a half of his crop, whereas the remaining portion is shared between landlord (another third to 40 per cent.) and Government (10 to 20 per cent.). The unsatisfactory state of dependence of tenant upon landlord, who, lacking interest in the actual work on the land, may evict him without notice, is aggravated by the fact that the landlord supplies the tenant with credit to cover the money needs of his farming, as a rule at the exaggerated rate of interest prevalent in Oriental rural areas. Heavy indebtedness, which often is passed on to the second generation, is the usual state of things in Oriental farming. It is only natural that reports of observers with a good inside knowledge of local conditions describe this situation in unmistakable terms. The following extracts are quoted at random from various sources :

SYRIA

"A large proportion of the emigration from the State of Syria may be traced to the inability of the Syrian peasantry to gain an adequate living in agricultural pursuits either as labourers or as proprietors. Wages of agricultural labour are very low because of its low productivity, and employment is seasonal. The use of primitive methods of cultivation has kept the productivity of the soil so low that even in good years the struggle for existence is difficult." (Said B. Himadeh, *Economic Organization of Syria*, Beyrouth, 1936, p. 15.)

LEBANON

The income of the peasant before the present war had become so restricted as scarcely to permit him to satisfy the most pressing needs of his family. This unhappy situation was not exclusive to the Syrian peasant, but was observed in certain regions of the Lebanon as well. In the course of an enquiry, conducted in 1938 upon the request of the Society for the Relief of Lebanese Artisans in a number of villages, it was found that the annual resources had fallen to 15 Lebanese pounds per person per annum, or 4 Lebanese piastres per day per head (i.e. less than one Palestine piastre). (Fouad Saadé in *L'Agriculture Richesse Nationale*, Beyrouth, 1942, p. 27.)

PALESTINE

"... the Fellah in Palestine has always been, until recently, the subject of oppression, neglect, and ill-treatment by his own countrymen and the old political régime. The feudal system played havoc in his life, the effendi class looked down upon him, and the old Turkish régime was too corrupt to be concerned with such a vital problem." (Afif J. Tannous in *The Open Court*, 1935–6, p. 236.)

CYPRUS

In Cyprus 82 per cent. of all peasants are in debt. The average debt of debtors is £36.

"But money-lending is not confined to the capitalist in the towns. The more well-to-do peasant with a little money to spare is equally insistent on his pound of flesh and, since he is often the only source of credit open to the poorest peasant, his demands are usually greater and more unconscionable." (Vide B. J. Surridge, in *Survey of Rural Life in Cyprus*, Nicosia, 1930, pp. 37 and 46.)

TURKEY

Even in modern Turkey, where industrialization is progressing remarkably, agricultural conditions have failed to keep pace with the general development of the country. Recent observers attribute the existent backwardness of the peasant and his indebtedness (pre-war conditions) to the preoccupation of the young republic with its industrial programmes. Despite repeated allotments of state and church lands to farmers, half of the peasantry still appear to be without any land of their own.

Yet even after giving due weight to conditions of land tenure, it would be unwise to neglect the question of productivity as being of particular importance to Oriental agriculture.

CHAPTER V

THE STANDARD OF PRODUCTIVITY IN ORIENTAL ECONOMY

As it is not possible here to give a detailed description of the economic conditions of all Oriental countries, we shall try to demonstrate one of the most important aspects of Oriental economy in terms of productivity per worker. By this we understand the compound value of the annual net production of an economic sector as a whole divided by the number of the workers (earners) occupied therein. More than any complicated analysis or lengthy comparison of economic conditions in Western and Middle Eastern countries, productivity data may serve as key figures for the understanding of the gap existing between the production standards of both regions, enabling us to suggest expedients for bridging this difference in economic development. In view of the predominance of agriculture in the economic structure of the majority of these countries, the productivity per worker in agriculture may to a large extent be regarded as representative of the average income of the bulk of the population.

1. Agricultural Productivity in the Middle East and Elsewhere

To obtain internationally comparable statistics in the sense used, we have to calculate the net output per male worker, i.e. production exclusive of fodder and fertilizer consumption. We prefer to take into account male workers only, since the various countries providing data on earners have failed to conduct their records on uniform lines as regards the registration of female labour. As Mr. Clark, in his *Conditions of Economic Progress*, has established an international unit to serve as a measuring rod for comparing the productivity and income of earners in the different occupations and countries, we can profitably use the said unit for our purpose. This " International Unit " is defined as the amount of goods and services that could be purchased for $1 in the U.S.A. over the average of the decade 1925–34. The " International Price " corresponds to the average price received by farmers for each commodity in dollars in the U.S.A. over the average of the decade 1925–34.

The computations were made in the following manner : At

first the net output for the whole country was calculated, attention being paid to the fact that a substantial proportion of the agricultural produce is again consumed in the course of production by the livestock (fodder, grain) and by the land (manure). In the case of cereals, which serve as human food and as fodder for the livestock, only the human consumption has been taken into account. Statistics of agricultural produce in Oriental countries being even less reliable than those of Western territories, it was deemed appropriate not only to omit production figures of all vegetables and fruits other than potatoes, grapes, olives and citrus fruit, and to use this omission for balancing the value of repairs, depreciation of inventory and buildings, which was not deducted in the computation, but by no means infrequently to have recourse to our own estimates as well. Surpluses of exports or imports for human or animal consumption have likewise been added and deducted respectively with a view to obtaining the actual net output figure. As a rule, the aforementioned " International Prices " were used for the calculation of output values. These, it is true, occasionally lie above the prices prevailing in Middle East countries ; however, in order to achieve a comparison no choice was left. Only in the case of dates was the local export price taken. Mr. Clark has not included this commodity in his table, and so there was no need to take the price " abroad " for the sake of comparison.[1] As to production, the average of the years 1934 and 1935 has been selected for purposes of comparison with Mr. Clark's figures. It appears, however, that the figures arrived at are more or less representative for other years as well, in view of the relatively moderate fluctuations in crop yields during the last pre-war decade.[2]

[1] The price of American dates is several times that of Iraqi dates, which is apparently due to the difference in quality. In the case of oranges, however, the International Price was taken, although it was much higher (about double) than prices in Palestine and other Oriental countries; otherwise an international comparison would have been impossible. Only in the case of Palestine a second calculation was made, based on local prices (see note to table, † p. 47).

[2] Index of Crops (Average 1934–5 = 100).

	1929	1930	1931	1932	1933	1934–35	1936	1937	1938
Turkey . . .	88	78	90	73	94	100	122	114	135
Egypt . .	102	97	100	111	104	100	111	115	113
Syria and Lebanon .	109	111	90	67	74	100	91	103	128

TURAL AND PASTORAL PRODUCTION VALUED AT INTERNATIONAL PRICES AND NET PRODUCTIVITY PER M
AGRICULTURE, 1934–5

	Intern. Price.	Cyprus.	Palestine.	Syria.	Iraq.	E
	($ per quintal)			(in 1,000 International Units)		
s :						
Products	3·95	500	3,950	9,452	4,000	
ıeep, lambs, buffaloes, camels, pigs) *	24·7	965	741	6,125	10,739	
. . . .	50·6	366	653	3,183	3,103	
. . . .	56·6	214	311	3,537	3,565	
. . . .	31·7	300	1,141	1,323	700	
. . . .	57·6	74		618		
		2,419	6,796	24,238	22,107	
tion of Cereals :						
. . . .	3·27	1,815	6,096	16,292	16,543	
. . . .	6·94	117	1,110	1,457	4,650	
. . . .	3·31	300	621	1,614		
. . . .	1·90		42	247	300	
. . . .	2·32	232	464	1,740	928	
. . . .	2·41					
		2,464	8,333	21,350	22,421	
or Export (+) of Cereals for Human onsumption :						
. . . .	3·27	(−) 566	(−) 2,308	(−) 391	(+) 626	(−)
. . . .	2·41		(−) 99	(−) 1		
. . . .	2·32	(+) 146	(−) 264	(+) 193	(+) 3,713	(−)
. . . .	2·81	(+) 9		(−) 3		(−)
. . . .	1·90			(−) 18	(+) 8	(−)
. . . .	3·31	(+) 352	(−) 465	(−) 106		(−)
. . . .	6·94	(−) 117	(−) 1,100	(−) 1,324	(+) 60	(+)
. . . .	2·96			(+) 50		
		(−) 176	(−) 4,246	(−) 1,600	(+) 4,407	(+)

. . . .	0·63					
. . . .	5·80			9		7,7
. . . .	33·70	202		1,359	202	121,8
. . . .	2·48	1,393	714	5,028		4
. . . .	7·50	585	1,940	5,321		
, grapefruits	7·10	518	20,859	} 3,224	100	6,4
. . . .	7·30	66	80			6,6
. . . .	34·90	174	351	935	188	
. . . .	7·10	53				1
. . . .	19·20	36			} 200	2
. . . .	10·00	19	479	236		6
. . . .	2·62	99	127	1,079		6,3
§	5·25	147	199	2,122	63	17,7
. . . .	16·10	8		338	753	
. . . .	2·0	628				
. . . .	3·0				5,500	
		3,928	24,749	19,651	7,006	168,3
. . . .	3·83	(−) 23	(−) 477	(−) 57	(−) 1	(−) 18,8
nption :						
n seed	3·03	(−) 8		(−) 116		(−) 9,
ed	4·35	(−) 20				(−)
		(−) 28		(−) 116		(−) 9,
. . . .		8,584	35,155	63,466	55,940	308,5
aged in Agriculture		60,000	139,800	650,000	600,000	3,424,0
Iead in I.U.		143·1	251·5	97·6	93·2	90·1

the average price of beef and mutton.
urkey and Syria.
ginned. The price is determined on the basis that per each 35 quintals of cotton (ginned) there are 65 quintals of cott
seeds are $28.95 and $2.57 respectively. The total price (cotton + cotton seed) is : 28.95 + 4.75 = 33.7 ; [4.75 = $\frac{(65)}{(35)}$ 2.
gypt and Palestine.

¶ Export + 20%. (Local price.)

rice 1925–30 in U.S.A.
ge of 1934–5.
national de Statistique Agricole, Rome. Annuaire Statistique de la Société des Nations, Genève. Agricultural Statistics—I

The determination of the number of male earners represented a most complicated problem. Detailed statistics on occupational structure are available only in respect of Egypt, Turkey and Palestine. The data on other Oriental countries are, of necessity, based on estimates. Another difficulty to be contended with lies in the fact that a not inconsiderable part of the population of Iraq, Syria and Transjordan consists of nomadic tribes who are only for a part of their time or not at all engaged in an " earning " occupation. Their wholesale inclusion in the category of the " Occupied " would markedly decrease the average net output per head ; hence only a part of the Bedouins was included. It may further be contended that the number of earners in general, and particularly of male earners, in our tables exceeds that of the actually employed. It is quite possible that a proportion also of the settled earners registered in the censuses do merely part-time work, or are physically unfit for full work. Through their inclusion *in toto*, the average productivity per earner is of necessity reduced. Unfortunately there are no figures available as to the percentages of full, half-time and invalid workers. However, if we wish to ascertain the degree and average level of productivity attained by the agricultural community as a whole for purposes of comparison with conditions in other parts of the world, all earners, whether diligent or less diligent, fit or half-fit, have to be included.

The figures finally arrived at for these countries may therefore be liable to amendment ; but they are checked to the extent permitted by our present knowledge of the conditions prevalent in them.

As the foregoing table shows, there are very remarkable differences between the net productivity of the various Oriental countries, and that of other countries in the world. It appears that the average net output per male worker engaged in agriculture fluctuates between International Unit 252 for Palestine (average) as the highest, and 90 as the lowest, in respect of countries like Egypt, Iraq and Syria. Turkey, with I.U. 105, shows a somewhat improved position, but nevertheless belongs to the same group. Even Cyprus, which ranks considerably above the aforementioned countries, belongs to the same order of magnitude, with 144, compared to Palestine or the Western Hemisphere. If we exclude Palestine, the Arab sector of which has likewise not yet attained the standard of Western countries, we are justified in saying that the average productivity per male earner in Oriental agriculture is very much lower than that found in Western countries. It does not allow the people engaged in agricultural occupations more than a very meagre livelihood, which not infrequently remains below the minimum.

NET PRODUCTIVITY PER MALE EARNER OCCUPIED IN AGRICULTURE ON THE BASIS OF THE 1934–5 CROPS

Countries *	I.U.	Countries	I.U.
New Zealand	2 444	Palestine †	
Australia	1,524	Average:	252 (177)
Argentine	1,233	Arabs:	186 (148)
U.S.A.	661	Jews:	683 (371)
Holland	579	Cyprus	143
Germany	490	Turkey	109
Great Britain	475	Syria and Lebanon	98
France	415	Iraq	93
Poland	195	Egypt	90

* Figures in this column according to Colin Clark, *Conditions of Economic Progress.*
† Figures in brackets for Palestine have been calculated by taking into account local prices of citrus, which are far below the "international" citrus price (cp. footnote on p. 43).

The foregoing data are borne out by the family budgets of certain Oriental countries as described above; the yearly expenditure of a farmer's family of five stands there at an amount of about £25 to £30. This corresponds roughly to the actual net output of 90–109 I.U. per earner of a family with 1·5 male earners.

It should not be overlooked, however, that the very low productivity per male earner, which characterizes conditions in Oriental lands, refers to the *man* unit in agriculture. If we calculate the net productivity per unit of *land*, we obtain completely different figures for the same countries, as compared to those of productivity per man unit. There even exists a definite upward trend, as more men are employed on the unit of land. Thus, the highest productivity per unit of land is attained in those regions where irrigation necessitates the employment of a large number of working hands; and this explains the somewhat curious phenomenon in irrigated zones of an extremely low productivity per earner going hand in hand with very high figures of productivity per unit of land.[1]

NET OUTPUT PER HA. OF CULTIVATED LAND IN I.U.

Syria	40
Iraq	43
Egypt	128
Turkey	41
Palestine	39

[1] We have elaborated this problem in a separate chapter on the "Agricultural Absorptive Capacity of Oriental Countries," annexed hereto as Appendix I.

2. Industrial Productivity

It is far more difficult to obtain reliable and representative data on the standard of industrial productivity, i.e. net output per worker, in Oriental countries. We may take it for granted that the productivity of modern equipped industries in Oriental countries comes from the outset far closer to average European standards than does the agricultural output. Our comparative income figures of primary, secondary and tertiary occupations (vide pp. 17–18), though somewhat scarce, clearly demonstrate this fact. Agriculture, or primary industry, is very much dependent on local conditions ; the worker on the soil is in a sense himself a part of these conditions, which are shaped to a large extent by Nature. Modern influences have, as shown above, penetrated the sphere of Oriental agriculture only to a limited extent. Compared with this state of affairs, the sectors of manufacture, dominated, as they are, by the methods of modern mass production, i.e. by the use of large machine units and mechanical implements, represent a kind of transplanted economy. In contrast to the very modest capital outlay of the average farm unit in Oriental agriculture, practised in accordance with local conditions, huge sums relative to the number of occupied men are invested in industry.

According to an enumeration which covers part of the Egyptian industry,[1] the average investment per worker was £E.972. If we take the average investment in agriculture, we arrive for the primitive type of Fellahin farming only at a figure of about £E.40–100 in respect of total outlay, land excepted. Other Oriental countries show similar ratios. Nearly everywhere the average investment in industry is many times that in agriculture. Palestine, on the other hand, shows with regard to the Jewish agricultural sector that the average investment per earner in this entirely modernized branch approximates to, or even exceeds, the figure of investments in Jewish industry. We shall revert to this aspect of the problem.

It is principally this basic fact of " concentrated " capital outlay which is responsible for the so much higher productivity of modern industry, as compared with that in agriculture, and which explains the higher productivity, in terms of money, of the secondary industries over that of the primary ones. The average earning capacity not only of a worker in agriculture

[1] *L'Egypte Industrielle,* Feb. 1941, p. 26.

but even of an artisan is thus much inferior to that of a worker handling modern machinery which has involved a large capital outlay. But although fairly high productivity figures are the rule in the case of modern industrial establishments in Oriental countries, the fact must not be overlooked that rudimentary stages of industrialization still predominate in most of these territories.

(I) INDUSTRIAL NET OUTPUT PER WORKER OR PERSON EMPLOYED *
(Figures in $ at American prices, 1925)

	U.S.A.	Canada.	New Zealand.	Australia.	Hungary.	Estonia.
Net output	3,200	2,500	1,640	1,510	570	545

(II) GROSS AND NET OUTPUT *

	Number of Workers in 1,000s.	Gross Output per Head.	Net Output per Head.
Great Britain and Northern Ireland, 1907	7,354	£242	163·1
do. do. 1936	8,400	£342	246·6
France 1930	3,892	Frs.64,200 (£517·7)	25,700 (207·2)
Germany 1936	5,118	£574	294
United States 1937	8,569	£1,434	595

(III) OUTPUT DATA FOR MIDDLE EASTERN COUNTRIES †

	Number of Workers in 1,000s.	Gross Output per Head.
Egypt, 1941 (partial)	129·4	£E. 301
Turkey, 1938 "	100	LT. 2,610
do. 1934 "	70	LT. 2,660
Cyprus, 1938 "	3·4	LC. 271
Palestine, 1936—Jewish industries and handicrafts	30	LP. 303
Palestine, Jewish industries excl. handicrafts: 1930	6·8	£244
1933	13·9	£342
1937	19·7	£360

* Figures under (I) and (II) according to Colin Clark, *Conditions of Economic Progress*, pp. 278, 287, 290, except those for Germany and U.S.A. The latter are computed from L. Rostas, " Industrial Production, Productivity and Distribution, etc. " in *Economic Journal*, April, 1943.

† Own computations according to census data ; mostly partial for Egypt, Turkey and Palestine ; the figure for 1936 is an estimate by L. Gruenbaum.

Calculations of output per worker or person employed in modern industries can, therefore, not be taken as indicating the average productivity of all earners in secondary occupations, the level of which is kept down by the large proportion of less-developed workshops and handicrafts. Besides, scarcely any published material is available as to the *net* output even of modern industrial plants.

Some figures, it is true, are available as to the gross output, but these are not very conclusive and merely serve to show the order of magnitude involved. As regards Egypt, for instance, we find, as a result of the partial enumeration mentioned above which embraced about half of the industries with 129,400 employed, that the gross output per earner in the establishments concerned amounts to £E.301 per annum; in Cyprus the relevant figure for the more developed industrial sector employing 3,389 workers is £271 *per capita.* There are two figures for Turkey which do not differ very much from one another. One derives from the Census of the so-called " encouraged " industries taken in 1934, which comprised 70,000 employed and showed an average gross value of production per earner of LT.2,610 per annum; the other from an enumeration of the " encouraged " industries in 1938, which arrived at LT.2,660 per annum in respect of 100,000 employed. In Palestine, the gross output of the Jewish industrial sector amounted in 1936, according to L. Gruenbaum, to LP.303 per earner. Other figures approximate to this one and appear to confirm that, given conditions of modern industrial production, the gross output per worker shows no great variations in principle, i.e. the potential productive capacity per earner in industry is more or less the same as in the more industrialized countries of the West. But there is one difference. The salary of the Oriental worker is far below that paid in Western countries owing to the different socio-political status of the worker in Oriental territories. Prior to the present war, the daily wages of a worker in industrial establishments amounted to 7·5–10 Piastres (= 1½ to 2 shillings) for unskilled and from 10 to 15 Piastres (= 2 to 3 shillings) in respect of skilled workers. Foremen used to receive even 5 or 6 shillings. Despite a rising productivity, which in modern establishments approaches the output figures of Western countries, the workers' remuneration lags far behind. From this point of view, the problem of achieving a higher standard of living could be solved far more easily in industry than in agriculture. For in the latter the objective conditions, i.e. the low productivity, must first be improved before any decisive change for the better can take place, whereas in the former the problem is solely one of social and wages policy.

However, the industrial sector will, for many years to come, remain second in importance as against agriculture, which employs the bulk of the Oriental population. As can be seen from the table below, the percentage of those engaged in secondary and tertiary occupations was in all Middle Eastern countries, Palestine excepted, less than a third of the total number of earners. As described above, the agricultural mode of life and hence rural living standards dominate the scene in all areas outside the actual urban centres.

The difference in the percentage of earners as between Turkey and Egypt, despite their almost identical populations, should be noted and probably finds its explanation in the differing definitions of the term "earner" by the census authorities of the two countries. To avoid any unduly large discrepancies between the figures concerned, it was deemed advisable, as already explained, to base the calculations of agricultural productivity on the number of male earners only (cp. page 42 and the tables on pages 44–45). The data for male agricultural earners in Egypt and Turkey correspond to the ratio between the total populations of these countries.

EARNERS ACCORDING TO CENSUSES

Country.	Total Population in 1,000s.	Total Earners in 1,000s.	Earners in Primary	Second.	Tertiary	Percentage I	II	III
			Occupations in 1,000s.					
Egypt (1937)	15,921	6,095	4,308	610	1,177	70·7	10·0	19·3
Turkey (1935)	16,158	7,921	6,480	656	785	81·8	8·3	9·9
Palestine (1931):								
Jews	175	66·5	12·3	19·6	34·6	18·5	29·5	52·0
Arabs *	861	212·1	122·3	27·1	62·7	57·7	12·7	29·6

CALCULATION OF EARNERS FOR 1934–5

Country.	Total Population in 1,000s.	Total Earners in 1,000s.	Earners in Primary	Second.	Tertiary	Percentage I	II	III
			Occupations in 1,000s.					
Egypt	15,170	5,879	4,156	588	1,135	71	10	10
Turkey	16,158	7,921	6,480	656	785	82	8	10
Syria	3,130	990	760	230		77	23	
Iraq	3,400	850	686	164		81	19	
Cyprus	360	137	81	56		59	41	
Palestine:								
Jews	310	130	25	105		19	81	
Arabs *	929	232	132	100		57	43	
Transjordan	300	75	60	15		80	20	

* Includes also negligible numbers of non-Arabs and non-Jews.

CHAPTER VI

PROGRESS THROUGH PLANNED DEVELOPMENT

Our results so far are clear. The living conditions of the vast majority of Oriental populations are exceedingly depressed. There exists a gulf between their standards of living, of education and of health and those of Occidental peoples. It is perhaps only the indigenous population of the densely settled areas of Eastern Asia and India that may be considered as being on the same low level as regards the satisfaction of human needs. In the world of to-morrow, nay of to-day, this state of things is rightly held as a challenge to modern concepts of society. Moreover it appears that the peoples in question will not for ever acquiesce in their destiny nor go on playing the rôle of destitute masses, but will claim their share in the wealth of the world.

It has been established by us that the very low productivity in agriculture is one of the main reasons for the low level of real income and of consumption. We have seen, in addition, that an enormous share of the peasant's income is claimed by the landowner and by all kinds of middlemen at the various stages of production and distribution, and this factor, coupled with the rate of interest charged for rural debts, accounts for the smallness of the peasant's share. There is, further, the appalling state of health and hygiene in general. Finally, the intellectual capacities of the Oriental masses are vastly under-developed and in great need of improvement, both quantitatively and qualitatively. No progress is possible unless there is a change for the better in all these spheres.

Now it may well be that some of the worst sources of evil for the physical well-being of the Oriental populations could be eliminated by a bold and far-flung hygiene and health policy, provided this is maintained in the face of disappointments and setbacks. It is further conceivable that the dissemination of elementary education and vocational training may ultimately lead to an improvement in methods of farming and a consequent rise in the income of the peasant. However, in view of an annual average income of about £5 per head of the rural population, these measures should not be overrated, as they will not be able to bring about any decisive change in the prevailing standard of living.

We are therefore driven towards a more radical policy such

as would scarcely have been recommended by social reformers of earlier days. The introduction of a policy of this kind involves, however, a determinate attitude on the part of Government, which in turn is contingent on far-reaching changes in economic-political conceptions and in the political structure of the countries concerned.

The following means are required to effect a definite improvement in the economic position of Oriental populations :

First, a redistribution of the present national income through increased taxation, the latter to be used for expanding state services and reducing the prevailing interest and rent charges. It is true that a redistribution of income is not in itself sufficient to induce any rise in the total income. Yet the fact remains that such a redistribution of income, which would include new state services for the benefit of the masses, induces a far better allocation of the social product, as can be seen from the following schematic calculation (the total in both cases being the same) :

PER CAPITA DISTRIBUTION OF REAL INCOME

Case A : Extreme Inequality :		
10,000,000 recipients of income at	£10	= £100,000,000
100,000 „ „ „ „	£1,000	= £100,000,000
		£200,000,000
Case B : Improved Redistribution :		
10,000,000 recipients of income at	£15	= £150,000,000
100,000 „ „ „ „	£500	= £ 50,000,000
		£200,000,000

The second means, which must exert a far more decisive effect towards material improvement, is that of an all-round and permanent increase in the real income per head of the working population. The rise in the real *per capita* income of a nation is virtually identical with an increase in the net output per head through expansion and intensification of agriculture, industrialization, and the development of transport services to decrease marketing costs. This would in no way render a redistribution of income superfluous ; linked to it, moreover, it would constitute a powerful combination to effect definite progress towards the goal of a higher standard of living. As there is a natural limit to the capacity of consumption of the necessities of life (food, etc.), particular attention must be paid to industrialization, consumption prospects in this sphere being practically unlimited for a long time to come. Machine production and intensified agriculture both lead to a marked increase in the national product available for sharing out, and when these are accompanied by adequate measures for equalizing distribution, such as taxation with a view to expanding state services, reduction of rent and interest, modern wages policy, and reform of land tenure, important preconditions are fulfilled to achieve the objectives aspired to.

Another by no means irrelevant expedient would lie in the raising of the exchange value of primary (agricultural) products as against secondary and tertiary ones. The present ratio, if expressed in terms of remuneration of agricultural and industrial workers for the same working time, is about 1 : 3, i.e. the latter earn about three times more than the former. If the price of the agricultural produce rises, as it will do following the shifting of workers from the primary to secondary and tertiary occupations as a result of industrialization, the agricultural producer will enjoy a higher purchasing power of his income, i.e. a higher real income than before.

Finally, as the real income per earner increases by the measures referred to above, a simultaneous demand for tertiary products (services, communications, administration, recreation, etc.) will grow rapidly, and numerous new sources of livelihood will spring up, absorbing a considerable part of the annual population increase at a fairly high standard of living.

To summarize : Planning of progress in Oriental countries with the principal end of a general rise in the standard of living has to aim at

(1) Increased agricultural production and productivity per earner through the intensification of agriculture and the extension of the land under cultivation ;
(2) A change in the ratio of prices between agricultural and industrial goods in favour of the former ;
(3) Large-scale production of industrial goods (industrialization), including the provision of better housing ;
(4) Development of public services (health, education, transport, etc.).

We shall now deal with the various problems involved in the policies outlined above, having regard at the same time to the issues of equalizing income which are closely connected therewith.

To prove the feasibility of our deductions and conclusions it was necessary to prepare a number of calculations and estimates, although it was clear from the outset that fully reliable source material such as is found in Western countries is not yet available here. However, the of-necessity-somewhat-hypothetical nature of a number of our findings and their dependence on certain political, biological and technical assumptions is a feature they share with many contemporary planning schemes. For the same reason it is evident that the deductions and conclusions summarized below do not offer any prognosis. They are an attempt to demonstrate potential development under certain conditions.

1. Increased Agricultural Production and Productivity per Earner through the Intensification of Agriculture and the Extension of the Land Under Cultivation.

Industrialization as an important factor in raising the income level of extensive sections of the population has, it is true, a first claim on our reconstruction thought. But it is not sufficient to secure an in all respects satisfactory solution for our problem of the development of Oriental territories. Industrialization cannot be forced ; it finds certain, at least temporary, restrictions in the availability of entrepreneurs and capital as well as in the adaptability and willingness of the workers, in unfavourable conditions of transport, and in the psychological readiness or otherwise of the masses to acquire new habits of consumption. There are certain considerations from which it appears that the introduction of public works raises the income more easily. However, public works executed in an unbroken sequence call for an expenditure of finances that is beyond the powers even of wealthier states. Hence we have to take into account all the opportunities within the realm of agriculture itself, such as increase of productivity and extension of cultivated area which would subsequently afford a rise in standard of living. Here as well we have to examine from various angles whether such an increase in output is at all feasible. Purely technical questions connected with the enhancement of productivity cannot be gone into here, but we may rest assured, on account of much experience in Middle Eastern countries, that they are well soluble.

The economic problems involved are :

(*a*) the capacity for increasing the consumption of agricultural products or, alternatively, the suitability of the latter for competition on foreign markets ;

(*b*) the availability of land necessary for the increase in production ;

(*c*) the presence of the labour required in connection with the increased activity ;

(*d*) the availability of capital necessary for the increase in production either through its intensification or by extending the cultivated area.

We shall analyse these prerequisites in the order indicated above with the exception of item (*d*), which is treated in a separate chapter.

(*a*) : The quantitative human consumption of elementary foodstuffs on the whole appears to have reached a limit even in Oriental countries. But this is only a half-truth. Our considerations have to start from facts the knowledge of which has become more and more common during the past two decades. The results of modern nutritional study have demonstrated that all countries show a remarkable under-consumption of certain vital foodstuffs. This is true not only of countries in which there are special reasons for difficulties in balancing the foodstuffs budget of the masses. The gap between nutritional norm and actual nutrition is exceptionally great even in a country like the United States, which heads the lands with satisfactory nutritional conditions. The modern theory of nutrition considers it vital that the *per capita* consumption of so-called protective foods, i.e. those foodstuffs which contain proteins and vitamins such as milk products, eggs, citrus and other fruits and vegetables should not drop below a certain level. New computations for the population of the United States have proved that in order to secure this minimum the production of milk in the U.S.A. must be increased by 33 per cent., that of eggs by 25 per cent. and that of vegetables by 90 per cent.[1] It will be impossible to produce such an increase without a very considerable change in the structure of American agriculture, which is still largely devoted to export production. The theoretical absorptive capacity of the United States alone for agricultural products of this kind is therefore very far from exhausted.

Another computation published by the U.S. Bureau of Agricultural Economics shows likewise considerable gaps between the actual crop acreage and the actual number of livestock for domestic use and the required acreage and number of livestock for " best adapted diet ".[2] The figures below show the differences in respect of livestock.

[1] A. Hansen and C. P. Kindleberger in *Foreign Affairs*, April, 1942.

[2] U.S. Bureau of Agricultural Economics: Estimates of Quantities of Food Necessary to Provide Certain Specified Diets and Crop Acreages and Numbers of Livestock Required for Indicated Production. Statement prepared by O. V. Wells and submitted on February 13, 1942.

Commodity.	Actual Number of Livestock for domestic use 1936–40.	Required Number of Livestock for "best adapted diet".	
	Millions.	Millions.	Increase in %.
Milk cows	23·9	33·3	39
Hens (for eggs)	369·0	452·9	23
Meat animals slaughtered :			
Sheep and lambs . .	21·9	25·5	16
Hogs	60·5	69·3	15
Chickens	644·0	699·5	9
Beef cattle	15·2	16·2	7
Veal calves	9·6	10·1	5

According to Sir John Boyd Orr, conditions in Great Britain are similar, protective foods being consumed much less than is desirable. To bring liquid milk consumption up to the level recommended by the Advisory Committee on Nutrition and approved by the Government in 1935, production would need to be nearly doubled. This would necessitate a reorientation of agriculture towards the production of foods which can be produced at home as economically as they can be imported.[1]

The rise in the consumption of liquid milk would leave little milk for making butter and cheese, and imports of these would need to be increased to make good the deficiency in home production and to raise the total supply to the higher level of consumption required for a health basis. If the additional requirements for fruit are found to be of the same order as those for the United States, namely 70 per cent., augmented imports, together with increased home production, would have to provide the necessary amounts. The larger dairy cow, pig, and poultry populations would call not only for an extension of home-grown fodder crops, but also for an increase in the amount of concentrates for feeding-stuffs, the imports of which in pre-war days amounted to about 8½ million tons per annum. An agricultural nutrition policy thus calls for both increased production and increased imports.

The same applies with even greater weight to the population of the Middle East countries. Here the deficiency in the consumption of vital foodstuffs, taken against the level calculated

[1] Sir John Boyd Orr, "The Rôle of Food in Post-war Reconstruction," *International Labour Review*, March, 1943.

as adequate, is so large that we reach virtually unimaginable figures if we calculate the *per capita* deficit for the population of all Oriental countries. A milk production sufficient for covering the need for proteins customarily supplied from milk would require the introduction of many hundred thousands of cows, as the following table shows.

ACTUAL AND OPTIMUM CONSUMPTION OF THE RURAL POPULATION OF THE MIDDLE EASTERN COUNTRIES [1]

(Population figures for 1939–
Quantities are given in 1,000 tons, when not otherwise stated.)

Country.	Egypt.	Turkey.	Palestine.		Iraq.	Syria and Lebanon.	Trans-jordan.	Cyprus.
			Arabs.	Jews.				
Rural Population (1939) (in 1,000s)	13,700	14,600	700	130	2,100	2,500	240	300
Meat and Fish:								
optimum . . .	300	320	15	3	46	55	5	7
actual	154	165	8	2	24	28	2	3
Vegetables:								
optimum . . .	1,750	1,865	89	16	268	319	31	38
actual	1,105	1,178	57	16	169	202	19	24
Fruits:								
optimum . . .	1,000	1,066	51	9	153	183	17	22
actual	720	767	37	8	110	131	13	16
Bread (wheat):								
optimum . . .	*2,110	2,248	108	20	323	385	37	46
actual	1,055	3,329	87	21	260	340	45	61
Milk and Milk products (1,000 tons):								
optimum . . .	3,000	3,197	153	28	460	546	53	66
actual	1,250	2,119	64	14	192	228	22	27
Eggs (1,000 units):								
optimum . . .	2,534,500	2,701,000	130,000	24,050	388,500	462,500	44,400	55,000
actual	822,000	876,000	42,000	32,890	126,000	150,000	14,400	18,000
Oils and Fats:								
optimum . . .	200	213	10	2	31	36	3	4
actual	400	426	20	3	61	73	7	9
Sugar:								
optimum . . .	400	426	20	4	61	73	7	9
actual	250	266	13	3	38	46	4	5

* The average *per capita* consumption of wheat and wheat flour in Egypt is far below that of the surrounding countries, the reasons being that the rural population of Egypt consume large quantities of maize and rice.

[1] *Sources.*—Optimum Diet computed from reports of various authoritative Nutrition Commissions, on the assumption that the food requirements are the same for the peoples of all lands and races (Orr).

Actual Diet, according to (*a*) estimates for Palestine Arabs in "An Inquiry into the Diets of various sections of the Urban and Rural Population", *Bulletin of the Palestine Economic Society*, Nov. 1931, Table XVIII; and (*b*) W. Cleland, *The Population Problem in Egypt*, p. 120; (*c*) Wheat consumption according to estimates of the *Bulletin of the Economic Research Institute*, J.A. No. 2, 1942; (*d*) Milk consumption in Turkey according to F. Eppenstein, *Das türkische Volkseinkommen*, Prag, 1893.

Although our figures cannot pretend to be based on comprehensive *enquêtes*, they should nevertheless be regarded as a cautious estimate. An investigation mentioned by an Egyptian author arrives at figures of actual consumption which, in respect of important food items, are much lower than those quoted in the table.

ACTUAL CONSUMPTION IN EGYPT PER CAPITA

Our Estimate.		Figures quoted by Mr. M. Boultros Gali.[1]	
Wheat	77 kg. per year		71 kg. per year
Meat and Fish . .	31 gr. per day	Meat only . .	14 gr. per day
Sugar	50 gr. per day		20 gr. per day
Milk (incl. all milk products) . .	250 gr. per day		47 gr. per day

The position appears to be fairly good in the case of animal and vegetable fats, where actual consumption exceeds the optimum, but tremendous deficiencies exist as regards the adequate supply of eggs, meat, cheese, fruits, vegetables, etc. Here, too, the question is one of expanding production to a degree which seems almost unreal in comparison with present conditions, and this despite the fact that no consumption figures have been included in respect of the urban population, large sections of which surely cannot boast of any higher nutritional standards.

Naturally these consumption figures cannot, in the very nature of things, be regarded as a binding norm. They represent an optimum rather than a real goal. Plans for the development and opening up of agriculture cannot count on eliminating the heritage of generations within any brief period of time. They are used here merely as an indication of the order of magnitude involved during a period of some decades ; and it is clear that even a partial improvement in consumption of protective foods would permit of an enormous rise in production. This would apply even if nothing more than local consumption were considered. But we need not limit our calculations of marketing prospects to the demands arising out of the need for increased consumption in Oriental countries alone. The change of consumption habits in the world will enhance the export prospects of Middle Eastern produce, which will also favourably affect production.

For a long time the consumption of cereals has no longer

[1] M. Boultros Gali, *The Policy of To-Morrow* (Arabic), 1938.

risen; indeed, there are certain countries in which the rise in the general standard of living has been accompanied by a falling-off in the consumption of bread. The elementary foodstuffs which play so important a part in the families of the under-privileged classes, are supplemented as living standards improve, or else replaced by richer or more expensive foodstuffs such as meat, milk, cheese, eggs, fruit and vegetables. There is a particularly narrow range of elasticity in the demand for cereals, sugar and potatoes, whereas the potential demand for milk, eggs and vegetables is considerable. Hence an increase in income may be expected to lead to an increased demand in precisely these commodities. The changes in cultivation called forth by such an international change in requirements can nowhere be undertaken with such relative ease as in the countries of the Orient. Here land, sun and water are available in large quantities, enabling farming to be based on intensive and more profitable branches instead of grain production. From the viewpoint of international demand, a favourable prognosis can thus be offered as far as the marketing prospects of the "protective" foods are concerned. With the exception of dates, the present share of Oriental countries in the supply of the world market with these products is still so limited, relatively speaking, that an increase, which for the producing countries would mean a considerable rise in output, would be easily absorbed on the world market.

EXPORT FROM ORIENTAL COUNTRIES AS PERCENTAGE OF WORLD EXPORT (1938)[1]

	Palestine.	Syria.	Turkey.	Iraq.	Egypt.	Total.
Oranges, tangerines, etc.	22·6	1·1	0·2	—	0·7	24·6
Lemons	—	3·7	—	—	—	3·7
Grapes	—	1·0	0·1	—	—	1·1
Raisins	—	0·2	22·1	—	—	22·3
Onions	—	3·6	—	—	23·7	27·3
Potatoes	—	0·3	—	—	—	0·3
Dates	—	—	—	74·9	0·2	75·1
Eggs	—	1·6	0·8	—	0·6	3·0
Rice	—	—	—	0·1	0·8	0·9

From the foregoing list a number of essential products have been omitted as, for instance, groundnuts, which have proved very valuable for oil production during the war but may become less competitive under changed post-war conditions. On the

[1] *International Yearbook of Agricultural Statistics*, 1938–9.

other hand, some most important agricultural products must be added, being invaluable as raw materials for processing industries :

EXPORT FROM ORIENTAL COUNTRIES AS PERCENTAGE OF WORLD EXPORT (1938) [1]

	Palestine.	Syria.	Turkey.	Iraq.	Egypt.	Total.
Cotton	—	0·1	0·9	1·3	12·8	15·1
Cottonseed	—	0·2	0·3	1·0	42·8	44·3
Cottonseed oil	—	—	—	—	11·5	11·5
Silk	—	0·2	0·4	—	—	0·6
Olive oil	0·7	4·3	2·1	—	—	7·1
Tobacco (leaves)	—	0·3	7·0	—	—	7·3
Sugar	—	—	—	—	0·4	0·4

Here as well the share of Oriental countries in the supply of the world market is negligible and, except for cottonseed, permits of a considerable increase, more especially if the *per capita* consumption all over the world increases as the rising standard of living makes itself more and more felt.

It should be interesting to complete this analysis by a calculation of the degree of self-sufficiency in Oriental countries at the present level of average productivity. For this purpose we shall have to calculate the output of foodstuffs, including the output of fruits and vegetables and to add or deduct the net import or export of foodstuffs. To give a complete picture of agricultural output, the consumption figures thus arrived at require to be refined by taking into consideration the net import or export of such agricultural produce as does not serve as food for man or beast. The final figures in respect of our Oriental countries then show the extent of dependence on foreign sources by relating output to consumption.

As regards Palestine, the ratio between production and consumption of foodstuffs (excluding oranges, which are chiefly exported) goes to show that the population of this country is far from being self-sufficient. To achieve self-sufficiency, a large amount of additional labour to make up the deficit would be required on the assumption, of course, that the additional food can be produced at fairly competitive prices. In other Middle Eastern countries the difference between output and consumption is not very marked as far as articles of food are concerned. On

[1] *International Yearbook of Agricultural Statistics*, 1938–9.

the other hand, the production of industrial raw materials from the vegetable kingdom is likely to change the ratio by increasing the output, the value of which would then exceed by far that of consumption. In Egypt, for instance, the production of cotton for export is reflected in the comparatively large excess of output over consumption.

As may be seen from the following table, the present consumption of agrarian produce in a number of countries already claims the total production, i.e. the total labour at present available in agriculture. A policy pursued for the purpose of raising revenue and consumption, would involve either a considerable increase in the number of workers or a rise in the average productivity, very probably both.

OUTPUT AND CONSUMPTION OF AGRICULTURAL PRODUCE ON THE BASIS OF THE 1934–5 CROPS

Country.	Output and Consumption of Foodstuffs in 100,000 I.U.				Consumption per Head in I.U.	Output and Consumption of Agricultural Produce other than Foodstuffs in 100,000 I.U.			Consumption per Head in I.U.	Ratio of Output to Consumption.	
	Recorded Output of Foodstuffs.	Output of Various Fruits and Vegetables as far as not included in(1).	Net Import (+) or Export (−)	Total Consumption.		Output of Agricultural Produce other than Foodstuffs.	Net Import (+) or Export (−).	Total Consumption.		Foodstuffs (1 + 2) : 4.	Foodstuffs and other Produce (1+2+6):(4+8)
	(1)	(2)	(3)	(4)	(5)	(6)	(7)	(8)	(9)	(10)	(11)
Egypt . . .	2,110	300	+ 41	2,451	16·0	1·259	− 1,108	151	0·98	0·98	1·41
Turkey . . .	3,139	298	− 372	3,065	19·3	538	− 148	390	2·45	1·12	1·18
Syria	564	100	− 45	619	19·0	72	− 6	66	2·03	1·07	1·07
Iraq	512	26	− 83	455	13·8	47	− 26	21	0·63	1·18	1·23
Cyprus . . .	79	8	− 9	78	21·5	8	− 2	6	1·59	1·12	1·14
Palestine . . .	349	44	− 20	373	30·1	7	+ 10	17	1·36	1·05	1·03
do. (figures excluding oranges)	143	44	+ 154	341	27·5	7	+ 10	17	1·36	0·55	0·54
do. Jewish sector .	28	9	+ 91	128	41·3	0	+ 6	6	2·14	0·29	0·28
do. Arab sector .	115	35	+ 63	213	22·9	7	+ 4	11	1·13	0·70	0·70

(*b*) : In the following we propose to deal with the availability of land for further extension of the cultivated area as well as the intensification of agriculture. We have already mentioned the fact that the areas of the Middle East comprise vast stretches of unused land to an extent probably unknown elsewhere in the Old World. But theirs is a special feature. Unlike countries in the temperate zone, the agricultural potentialities of the Middle East countries are largely dominated by the fact that they include substantial territories which require the use of artificial irrigation for the achievement of their maximum yields. Irrigated agriculture means the considerable additional application of capital and labour. But in return for this there is a manifold increase in productivity and a substantial expansion of yields per unit of area even compared to those zones where irrigated cultivation has been occasionally practised but has not yet reached its optimum.

The area on which irrigated farming can be practised in the Middle East may be estimated at approximately 132,000 square kilometres in Iraq, Palestine, Syria, Transjordan, Turkey and Egypt. Of this only 37,000 sq. kms. are at present cultivated under irrigation, in many cases by primitive and wasteful methods. Some countries show figures considerably lower than the general average for irrigated zones. Thus, for instance, in Iraq out of an estimated irrigable area of 51,000 sq. kms. only 7,000 sq. kms. are under irrigation. In Palestine, out of 4,000 sq. kms. 400 sq. kms. are actually irrigated.

The average agricultural density of population per square kilometre of irrigable land will not be too highly computed at 200. If the whole of the Middle East's irrigable but not yet

CLASSIFICATION OF MIDDLE EAST LAND ACCORDING TO UTILISATION, 1939
(in square kilometres)

Country.	Total Area.	Cultivable Area.	Cultivated Area.	Irrigable Area.	Irrigated Area.
Egypt	1,000,000	34,000†	24,000	34,000	23,000
Turkey	763,000	300,000	87,000	30,000	4,000
Iraq	453,000	92,000	13,000	51,000	7,000
Syria	202,000*	61,000	16,000	12,000	2,500
Palestine	27,000	12,000‡	9,000	4,000	400
Transjordan	90,000	4,600‡	3,500	600	200
Total	2,535,000	503,600	152,500	131,600	37,100

* Including the Alexandretta District; no separate figures are available as to the classification of land in that district.

† Including partly reclaimed area.

‡ Although there exist considerably higher estimates, a moderate figure has been inserted.

irrigated area is considered, this would indicate room for an additional population of 19,000,000. If for the purposes of a conservative estimate we assume that of the 95,000 sq. kms. of

Middle East irrigable but unirrigated land more than a third is worked under extensive cultivation and carries a population of 80 per square kilometre, the additional population figure might be computed at about 16,400,000.

On the other hand, we have not taken into consideration that of the unirrigable but cultivable lands of the Middle East a substantial part (some 257,000 sq. kms.) is still uncultivated.

Even on the lowest estimate, with a density figure of only 50 per square kilometre, the Middle East's unirrigable but cultivable land would provide room for an additional agricultural population of 12,850,000, and, together with the area of irrigation, the Middle East capacity for additional peasant population may be reckoned at approximately 30,000,000. On the other hand, the actual increase in population, urban and rural, in the coming two decades will, according to our estimates (p. 65), not exceed the number of 25 millions, if the present rates of increase are maintained. A problem of genuine shortage of agricultural living space within the whole of that region is therefore not at all likely to arise; this prognosis to hold good even if the increasing shift of the population from rural to secondary occupations, which are not limited by space, is disregarded.

(*c*) : As for procuring the labour necessary for the intensification and expansion of agriculture in Oriental countries, the following factors have to be borne in mind : (i) the rate of population increase and (ii) the willingness of the agricultural population to remain in its present occupation.

(i) To form an idea of the potential growth of population, we assume the continuation of the present rate of increase for the next twenty years and add it to the population figure of to-day. We then calculate the prospective shares of the three principal groups of occupations, assuming, further, that the shift from agriculture to industry and the services will, in most Oriental countries, leave a quota of between 57 and 77 per cent. in respect of primary producers. We then obtain the picture shown on the next page.

The percentage of earners in Egypt, Turkey and Cyprus is assumed to be on the decline, as the last censuses in these countries include a large number of children among earners. In future a growing percentage of children will attend schools and will, therefore, no longer be counted as earners.

While no certainty can be claimed for figures to be attained in 1962, they may nevertheless serve as an indication of the order

ASSUMED POPULATION AND EARNERS IN 1962 * (in 1,000)

Country.	Total Population as at 31 Dec. 1939.†	Assumed Total Population in 1962.	Assumed Total Earners in 1962.	Thereof in Agriculture		in Industry		in Services, Commerce, Transport, etc.		Male Earners in Agriculture.
				absolute.	%.	absolute.	%.	absolute.	%.	
Egypt	16,680	24,000	8,100	5,346	66	1,053	13	1,701	21	4,382
Turkey	17,620	26,000	12,000	8,160	68	1,680	14	2,160	18	4,760
Syria	3,700	5,500	1,800	1,080	60	306	17	414	23	840
Iraq	3,700	4,950	1,375	1,059	77	179	13	137	10	850
Cyprus	380	600	200	114	57	44	22	42	21	80
Palestine:										
Total	1,502	3,600	1,487	402	27	435	29	650	44	300
Arabs	1,057	1,500	500	260	52	80	16	160	32	208
Jews	445	2,100	987	142	14·4	355	36	490	49·6	92
Transjordan	300	450	150	113	75	18	12	19	13	90

* The year "1962" in our calculations represents the last year of our first development period of twenty years. The date in itself is of no particular importance; a change of the period would, of course, require some adjustments of figures in the table in view of the changes in the population.

† According to the *Statistical Yearbook* of the League of Nations, 1941–2.

of magnitude which may then be expected to prevail in the different categories of occupations. With regard to Palestine it has been assumed that the country may serve as a centre of attraction for a large number of Jews during the coming two decades. But even in case the number of Jews should not reach the figure assumed in the table, the general conclusions as to the other countries would not be affected thereby.

A share, in respect of rural occupations, of between 57 and 77 per cent. of total male earners would mean that the majority of Oriental countries will still remain predominantly agrarian in structure, although a percentage of 20 to 30 for male earners producing industrial goods and services already constitutes a long step towards industrialization. However, though reduced in proportion, the agricultural population, if taken in absolute figures, will be considerably larger in 1962 than in 1942.

Though this represents the general trend of occupational development in Oriental countries, certain deviations may be liable to occur as a result of factors, the effects of which are either at present barely or else not yet visible.

Some countries are already labouring under the difficulty of securing the amount of labour required in agriculture. In Iraq the intensification of cultivation is hampered in a number of areas by the lack of farm hands, a calamity which even an increase in wages has not yet succeeded in overcoming. If, in addition, a wave of industrialization should set in, an aggravation of the labour shortage, especially in the irrigated zones, will be unavoidable.

The position is different in countries like Egypt. Here the shifting of workers from rural occupations to urban callings may, it is true, reduce the percentage of those employed in agriculture. However, in view of the heavy rate of population increase, the absolute figure of those employed in agriculture would not be changed, and the scope of agricultural production could, therefore, easily be maintained. Notwithstanding this, a shortage of labour may arise here as well if the pace of industrialization should be too rapid, or if new agricultural development projects should increase the demand for labour. There are, according to Crouchley, vast stretches of newly reclaimed land in the north of the Delta, where development is actually held back owing to a scarcity of agricultural labour. Similar conditions prevail in a number of other Oriental countries. As a rule, no surplus labour is found to exist in rural districts, unless there have been radical changes in the organization of farm work. It is difficult to offer an exact prognosis for the balancing of these divergent trends, but there is reason to believe that the demand for agricultural labour will grow, if the drift from the village to the town persists at the rate of the past thirty years. A definite policy of industrialization and of intensification in agriculture, more especially in irrigated zones, must therefore include safeguards for the adjustment of claims on the labour reserve, in order to ensure that the schemes envisaged are carried out.

(ii) The willingness of the agricultural population to remain in their occupations depends, besides the conservatism of the "rural man", on whether conditions of life have or have not deteriorated as compared with other economic spheres. This, in turn, is connected with an important problem arising with special urgency in predominantly agrarian countries, such as those of the Middle East. It is the ratio between the values of agricultural and industrial products.

2. A Change in the Ratio of Prices between Agricultural and Industrial Goods in favour of the Former

The ratio between the values of agricultural and industrial goods provides a most significant aspect for gauging the prospects of agricultural development in Oriental countries. Experience gained in other countries goes to show that industrialization is apt to produce decisive changes in this ratio. Industrial mass production tends to cheapen the product even though the wages paid in industry may by far exceed those of agricultural labourers. The price of a machine-produced article is, as a rule, much cheaper than that of a hand-made one. Technical progress is apt to strengthen this tendency, as recent inventions in industry and applied technique have repeatedly proved. The development of communications may render profitable the exploitation of natural resources, which owing to the high costs of transport did not prove worth while previously. On the other hand, the shortage of labour in agriculture, caused by the shifting over to industry and the tertiary occupations, is bound to lead to a rise in the wages of agricultural labourers, and this in turn is apt to raise the cost-price of agricultural commodities. All this will bring about far-reaching changes in the terms of exchange of agricultural and industrial produce.

The Oriental countries will undoubtedly enter a stage of large-scale industrialization, and this process will coincide with an expansion of intensified and specialized farming. Both processes will have but one source of labour to fall back on, and it is no daring forecast to predict that in these circumstances the terms for agricultural produce will rise much more than those of industrial goods. Colin Clark, who devoted much thought to these trends, arrived at the figure of 1·85, being the new level for the value of agricultural products as against their former level, taken as 1, expressed in purchasing power over secondary and tertiary products. However, to be on the safe side, we assume, as mentioned above, an increase in the purchasing power of agricultural produce of only 50 per cent. over that of secondary and tertiary products, as against the level of 1934–5. In the same way, we assume a very modest increase in the net productivity per male earner which, as we have seen, ranged in 1934–5 between 90 in Egypt and 683 in the Jewish sector of Palestine. Disregarding the latter level as being fairly high, we shall again content ourselves with a rise of only 50 per cent. for all other countries. This rise, to be sure, does not include all improvements achievable through large capital investments, which may produce a more radical change in the level of productivity, in certain areas at least.

By way of conclusion from 1 and 2 we now proceed to determine the presumable total value of net agricultural production at the end of the period in question. As can be seen from the

AGRICULTURAL EARNERS IN 1934–5 AND 1962 AND THEIR NET OUTPUT

Country.	1934–5.			1962.					
	Male Earners in Agriculture	Total Net Production	Net Productivity per Head	Male Earners in Agriculture	Total Net Production according to 1935 [Price and Productivity Level	plus: Increase in Productivity 50%	plus: Increase in Exchange Value 50%	Total Net Production.	
	in 1,000s.	in million I.U.		in 1,000s.	in million I.U.			million I.U.	in £ million*
Egypt . . .	3,424	308·6	90·1	4,382	395	197	296	888	178
Turkey . .	3,354	366·4	109·2	4,760	520	260	390	1,170	234
Syria . . .	650	63·5	97·6	840	82	41	61	184	37
Iraq . . .	600	55·9	93·2	850	79	40	59	178	35
Cyprus . .	60	8·6	143·1	80	12	6	9	27	5
Transjordan .	60	5·4	90·1	90	8	4	6	18	4
Palestine :									
Arabs . .	121	22·6	186·3	208	39	19	29	87	17
Jews . . .	18	12·5	683·3	92	63	—	31	94	19
Total .	8,287	843·5	—	11,302	1,198	567	881	2,646	
Total Value in £ million .		168·7			239	113	177		529

*For the purpose of this calculation the value of £1 was put at 5 I.U.

above table, we arrive at a total value of about 2,646 million I.U. in respect of the agrarian production of our Middle East countries, as compared with 843 in 1934–5, or, expressed in pounds, of 529 million as against 169 million. Such a formidable rise will go a long way towards improving the standard of living of the Oriental rural population, despite the appreciable population increase which we expect will occur during the identical period.[1]

What is the meaning of this rise in terms of individual purchasing power? Take the case of an agricultural family of five which is maintained by 1·5 male earners (father and part-time working son) with an average net output of 90 I.U., the lowest in our scale. We then arrive at the scheme on the next page.

A family of five at the end of the period envisaged will therefore have at its disposal 303 I.U. as against 135 I.U. in 1935, provided, of course, that the monetary value remains unchanged.

[1] Even if we disregard the potential increase in exchange value, the final rise in purchasing power need not remain behind the figures quoted in the text. In lieu of the very conservative estimate of a 50 per cent. rise in agricultural productivity, an increase of 100 per cent. can safely be expected to result from the systematic application of modern methods and devices in Oriental farming.

Year.	Net Agricultural Productivity per Family (Holding).		Items of Expenditure.*			
			Household.		Other (rent, interest, saving).	
	Intern. Units.	£	I.U.	£	I.U.	£
1935	1·5 male earners × 90 = 135	27	125	25	53	10
1962	1·5 „ „ × 202 = 303	61	250	50	10–25	2–5

* Figures under this head refer to the expenditure of rural families as specified on page 25 and elaborated more fully on pp. 58 ff. There may be some occasional income from outside, i.e. non-agricultural sources, to cover excess of expenditure.

If the ratio of the I.U. to the pound sterling is 1 : 5, the value of the output will be £61 as compared to £27 in 1935. Part of this increase, it is true, will be drained away by the risen cost of food, the price increase of which constitutes one of the elements of the higher productivity of peasant agriculture. But the remaining surplus would still be substantial, as compared with the previous output value, and would enable the peasant to satisfy his needs for industrial produce. Here again stress must be laid on the fact that a 50 per cent. increase on a basic level of productivity of 90 I.U. (= £18) represents a very small rise indeed, the level in our example being the lowest imaginable. In the case of Syria and Turkey, where the original net output per male earner is about 100, the output per family may be expected to reach 330 and more in 1962, a level that would permit the consumption of a still greater amount of manufactured goods.

The subsequent chapter demonstrates the use to which this increased income should be put for raising the consumption level of the peasant population. This, in turn, constitutes one of the main factors of industrialization in a progressive economy.

3. Large-scale Production of Industrial Goods (Industrialization), including the Provision of Better Housing

The following review of prospects and limits of industrialization is offered in clear recognition of the fact that this is not a quick process which can be embarked upon overnight, but one that calls for a prolonged period for its realization and would be dependent upon a series of economic, political and sociological prerequisites. These comprise :

(*a*) The capacity for increasing the consumption of manufactured goods, housing included, or, alternatively, the suitability of such goods for competition on foreign markets ;

(*b*) The capacity for competition, i.e. the degree to which home products would be in a position to compete with foreign imports on the home market ;

(*c*) The presence of adequately trained and productive workers and technical staff,

(*d*) The availability of the capital necessary for the establishment of industry.

We propose to analyse these prerequisites in the order indicated above, (*d*) being again excepted, as this point will be treated in a separate chapter.

(*a*) : The capacity for increasing consumption of manufactured goods by the native populations of Oriental countries may be regarded as exceedingly high. In this connection two elements should be distinguished : the " physical " possibility of consuming more industrial manufactures and the economic possibility, i.e. the actual purchasing power of the population. As regards the physical capacity, we know from personal observations and numerous investigations that the present standard of living of the mass of the population, in our particular case the inhabitants of the villages, permits only a minimum consumption of industrial goods. The preponderant part of their income is needed for food (unmanufactured). However, any change in the size of the income is immediately followed by a change in the composition of the expenditure. Investigations of the relations of the individual categories of expenditure in various countries have shown that with rising income the share of the family budget used for food grows percentually less and, vice versa, that the expenditure on basic foodstuffs, which are generally the starch-containing cereals, plays a more important part in

Income in German Marks per Year.	Percentage of Income spent on Food.	Percentage of Income spent on Food, Clothing, Fuel and Medicines.
Under 525	66·2	101·3
525– 2,000 . .	61·9	93·3
2,000– 6,000 . .	42·0	69·8
6,000– 20,000 . .	26·0	57·6
20,000–100,000 . .	17·0	48·8
100,000 upwards	8·9	28·0

the budget as the income declines. This was established more than fifty years ago as "Engel's Law" and has since been repeatedly confirmed, with certain modifications, in the course of numerous inquiries. The table on the previous page contains the figures of Engel.

An inquiry in 1929 showed similar results for American conditions, as does a very recent study of the cost of living of the low-income classes in Palestine (Jewish families):

U.S.A.

Income Class.	Population (millions).	Average Income per Head.	Average Food Expenditure per Head.	Percentage of Income spent on Food.
		$	$	
I	0·73	25,100	550	2·2
II	2·19	3,975	320	8·0
III	7·17	1,800	265	14·7
IV	16·60	1,055	230	21·8
V	43·40	568	175	30·8
VI	51·40	211	105	49·8

From *America's Capacity to Consume*, 1934.

PALESTINE

	Income Group I.	Income Group II.	Income Group III.	Income Group IV.
No. of Families	44	42	42	42
No. of Persons	230	172	155	139
For the year 1941:				
Average monthly income *per capita*	LP. 1·683	2·248	2·656	3·394
Average monthly expenditure *per capita*	LP. 1·854	2·368	2·713	3·023
Ratio of expenditure to income	110	105	102	89
Percentage of total income spent on food	70·3	61·6	60·8	50·6

A similar trend emerges when the data for one month only are examined (see Table, top of next page).

The same law, however, teaches that expenditure per head on foodstuffs is relatively inelastic in comparison with other categories of expenditure. In other words, with rising income

For February, 1942 :				
Average *per capita* income	LP. 1·920	2·360	2·915	3·413
Expenditure *per capita* on food	LP. 1·620	1·897	2·211	2·352
Percentage of income spent on food	84·4	80·3	75·8	68·9

From "Cost of Living of Low Income Groups among the Jewish Population of Palestine", *Bulletin of the Econ. Research Institute*, J.A., 1942, No. 4–6.

the tendency to increase consumption in clothing, furniture, equipment of the home, cultural and other requirements become stronger. This increased elasticity in the disposition of the balance of income left after acquiring foodstuffs has been repeatedly investigated, and certain trends have been observed, which are illustrated by the following table indicating the average income elasticity of demand for the principal commodities :[1]

AVERAGE PERCENTAGE OF FAMILY EXPENDITURE SPENT ON CERTAIN ITEMS AND AVERAGE INCOME ELASTICITY FOR THE SAME ITEMS[2]

	Food.		Clothing.		Furniture.		Rent.		Other Items.*	
	%	Income Elast.	%	Income Elast.	%	Income Elast.	%	Income Elast.	%	Income Elast.
Belgium, Workers (1928–9)	57	0·8	15	1·1	3	0·7	6	0·5	16	1·8
Germany, Workers (1927–8)	45	0·8	13	1·4	4	1·8	10	0·6	24	1·3
Finland, Workers (1920–1)	60	0·8	15	1·4	2	1·8	4·5	1·1	13·5	1·3
Czechoslovakia, Workers (1929)	58	0·8	10	1·4	3·5	1·3	5	0·9	18	1·5
Poland, Workers (1929)	56	0·45	17	1·6	3·5	2·2	4	0·6	15	2·3
U.S.A., all classes (1918)	38	0·8	17	1·4	5	1·2	13	0·7	22	1·3
Liverpool, Workers (1929)	47	0·9	8	1·4	—	—	21	0·8	15	1·7

* Excluding fuel and light.

The table shows that the income elasticity of food expenditure for the countries mentioned has remained below 1, whereas other items of expenditure such as clothing and furniture, etc., with their considerably higher elasticity co-efficient, point to a steeper increase in expenditure.

[1] Income elasticity is the ratio between the increment of consumption of a given commodity and an increment of income, other factors remaining constant (Allen and Bowley).

[2] From a table in *Family Expenditure*, by Allen and Bowley, 1935.

The Consumption Capacity for Household Goods in Oriental Countries

It is not possible to apply to the Oriental population direct the co-efficients of elasticity that are valid for European countries or Asiatic areas with other climates. However, a number of *enquêtes* into the standard of living as well as an inquiry into the distribution of expenditure of several hundred Jewish urban families in Palestine have shown that here, too, similar tendencies could be observed. Hence we may take it as well founded, when assuming the increase in the income and living standard of the Oriental population, that such an increase would primarily affect the expenditure on clothes, furniture, dwelling, education, etc. It is true that a rise in income also leads to an increased consumption of certain commodities within the "foodstuffs" category of expenditure, to which we shall return. This, however, may be ignored for the purpose of the present estimates. In the absence of data on the distribution of family expenditure in the various income classes of most Oriental countries, we are not yet in a position to compute a "co-efficient of elasticity" for them. Nevertheless, the available data offer a sufficient basis for gauging cautiously the prospective increase in consumption in the low-income strata. Here again, to be sure, the largest part of the income is claimed by food, which, according to the various *enquêtes*, absorbs 62·9 per cent. in Cyprus, 62·5 per cent. in Egypt, 69·9 per cent. in Arab Palestine. Among the remaining items of expenditure, clothing comes first.

Manufactured Goods Annually consumed in a Fellahin Household of Five [1]

Clothing	From	£E.	2·870	to	£E.	5·040
Beddings, blankets	,,	,,	1·000	,,	,,	1·250
Other items of consumption	,,	,,	1·060	,,	,,	1·240
In all	From	£E.	4·930	to	£E.	7·530
			Average £E. 6·230			

The expenditure on clothes of a village household in Egypt during 1931 amounted, according to our figures on page 25, to between £E.2·870 and £E.5·040 per family of five; that is, between £E.0·574 and £E.1·008 *per capita*.[2] The figures for Iraq or Syria, too, point to incredibly low sums for annual

[1] According to Cleland.

[2] We rely for our computations on figures showing conditions before the present war. Although this war has enriched the Fellah's farm to a large degree, "Easy come, easy go" will probably hold good this time as well. The "prosperity" of the last War and post-War period left scarcely a mark on the housekeeping and manners of life of the Fellahin once a few years had passed.

expenditure on clothing. We may justly consider that the Fellah can spend several times that amount. For other textiles (blankets, etc.) a sum of about £E.0·250 per head is entered in the family budget. Other articles of consumption (pots, dishes, soap, kerosene) require similarly trifling amounts. Hence it is an under-estimate rather than otherwise of the "physical" potentialities for increased consumption if we regard no more than a threefold increase of the present annual expenditure, namely £E.1·246 per head or £E.6·230 per family of five, as likely. This means, under Egyptian conditions, an additional family consumption of £E.12·460 for this class of industrial goods.[1]

This, however, in no way exhausts the potential consumption of industrial products The prospects of raising the consumption level, as mentioned hitherto, refer only to the few items that were already introduced as consumption goods in the peasant household. Even after this, however, there is still room for far-reaching reforms in the manner of life of the Oriental peasantry. As a rule the Fellah and his family sleep on the floor of their home, which is usually made of stamped earth. Very often they share this primitive accommodation with the cattle; although, as we have seen, such housing conditions could scarcely be worse from the hygienic viewpoint. If we assume that it would be possible to induce the Fellahin to use bedsteads instead of spreading their mats on the bare earthen floor, to utilize some kind of drainage measures, to increase the furniture of their homes, and finally to raise the hygienic and educational standard by acquiring schoolbooks for the children and medical articles, this would produce an additional rise in consumption of about £E.3 *per capita* and year, composed as follows:

OTHER NEWLY ADDED ITEMS OF CONSUMPTION

	Per Head. (£E.)	Per Family. (£E.)
Bedsteads, etc.	0·250*	1·250
Other purchases (such as furniture, sewing machine, other household goods, etc.)	1·750	8·750
Books and periodicals	0·200	1
Doctor, medicines, insurance	0·800	4
	3	15

* Assuming the period of use to be ten years.

[1] The relatively modest budget of a peasant in Cyprus, which stands probably between that of a peasant in Western Asia and a South European farmer, included in 1930 about £14 expenditure for "industrial" commodities, excluding allocations for house repairs. (See Surridge, *A Survey of Rural Life in Cyprus.*) A rise in the average expenditure of an Egyptian or Syrian Fellah to that standard does not, therefore, appear exaggerated at all.

Our estimated rise in personal requirements of about £E.12·460 should now be added to the above amount of 5 × 3 = £E.15; which would mean an increased expenditure per family amounting to roughly £E.27·500 or £E.5·500 per head. This would in any case constitute a doubling of the former standard, with a vast shift towards the so-called "secondary" expenditures. These tendencies are not theoretically contrived; they correspond to the actual course of the distribution of expenditure (the Law of Engel), according to which the expenditure on purposes other than foodstuffs begins to rise much more rapidly above a particular level of income than below. Assuming, in addition, that the rise in these expenditures will come not immediately but over an extended period, we are on sure ground; all the more so, as we do not expect that an increase in income as well will be noted otherwise than successively over a period of fifteen to twenty years.

The Consumption Capacity for Housing

This again does not exhaust our forecast as to the potential demand for industrial goods. So far we have considered only requirements deriving from personal expenditure, furnishing the home, etc. A far-reaching reform of housing conditions would be finally much more important, as well as far more accessible to collective planning, than changes in consumption affecting personal habits. In view of the magnitude of the objective it is evident that such planning will, taken year by year, comprehend only fractions of the total plan, the full execution of which would take, say, twenty years. The following considerations underlie our calculations of housing requirements: first, the growth of population since 1939 has to be taken into account, Further, a rate of 33·3 per cent. has been assumed for the entire period of twenty years as giving the need for rebuilding existing houses. In order to illustrate the magnitude involved in the matters dealt with here, the price for the provision of a new house for the rural population is tentatively set at £E.15 per head.[1] Distributing requirements over twenty years, this means that, theoretically speaking, a total of £421 million or £21 million per annum, would require to be expended on the rural populations of the countries listed below.

[1] Proposals suggesting an outlay of £E.30 per family in respect of rural housing had already been made in Egypt. An amount of £E.15 per head appears, however, to be the minimum for a scheme which aims at genuine improvement.

ASSUMED TOTAL INVESTMENTS IN RURAL BUILDING DURING THE YEARS 1943–62, AND ANNUAL AVERAGE [1]

Country.	Rural Population			Number of Old and New Rural Population in Need of Housing.			Assumed Investments in Rural Building.	Assumed Annual Average Investment.
	On 31st December, 1939.	In 1962.	Percentage of total population.	New demand 1939–62.	Replacement demand.	Total.		
	(in millons)			(in millions)			(in £ million)	(in £ million)
Egypt	13·7	19·7	82	6·0	4·8	10·8	162	8·10
Syria and Lebanon	2·5	3·8	69	1·3	0·8	2·1	31·5	1·58
Palestine . . .	0·8	2·0	55	1·2	0·3	1·5	22·5	1·13
Turkey	14·6	21·6	83	7·0	4·9	11·9	178·5	8·92
Iraq (excl. nomads)	2·1	2·7	72	0·6	0·7	1·3	19·5	0·98
Cyprus	0·3	0·45	75	0·15	0·1	0·25	3·8	0·19
Transjordan . .	0·24	0·36	80	0·12	0·08	0·20	3·0	0·15
Total . .	34·24	50·61	79	16·37	11·68	28·05	420·8	21·05

ASSUMED INVESTMENTS IN URBAN BUILDING DURING THE YEARS 1943–62, AND ANNUAL AVERAGE [1]

Country.	Urban Population			Number of Old and New Urban Population in Need of Housing.			Assumed Investments in Urban Building.	Assumed Annual Average Investment.
	On 31st December, 1939.	In 1962.	Percentage of total population.	New demand 1939–62.	Replacement demand.	Total.		
	(in millions)			(in millions)			(in £ million)	(in £ million)
Egypt	3·0	4·3	18	1·3	1·0	2·3	161	8·05
Syria and Lebanon	1·2	1·7	31	0·5	0·4	0·9	63	3·15
Palestine . . .	0·7	1·6	45	0·9	0·2	1·1	77	3·85
Turkey	3·0	4·4	17	1·4	1·0	2·4	168	8·40
Iraq	0·8	1·1	28	0·3	0·27	0·57	39·9	2·00
Cyprus	0·1	0·15	25	0·05	0·03	0·08	5·6	0·28
Transjordan . .	0·06	0·09	20	0·03	0·02	0·05	3·5	0·17
Total . .	8·86	13·34	21	4·48	2·92	7·40	518·0	25·90

Of this total of roughly £21 million per annum on rural building some 25 to 30 per cent. would fall to industrial goods ; a percentage which would increase with an improved standard of housing and equipment by the use of wood and metal for windows and doors, and plumbing. In the case of urban resi-

[1] The year 1943 is taken as the first year in which building activities will commence. If a later date is taken as a point of departure, slight modifications must be inserted.

dential building, or building for industrial purposes, it amounts on an average to far more than in rural building, and over the whole country reaches at least 40 per cent. Hence these sources provide very considerable opportunities for industry. If we now add to the cautiously estimated sums for rural housing a housing demand of about £70 per head of the urban population, we find, given a period of twenty years, that a further sum of £518 million or an annual average of £26 million will be required. In taking as a basis the population of 1939, we have to consider the growth of population since then, while, on the other hand, we assume, as in the case of rural housing, a rebuilding of dwelling-houses to the extent of 33·3 per cent. in the course of twenty years; although it is quite possible that a far greater part of the available houses fall away or require to be rebuilt. For the purpose of this calculation we also neglect the important orders that will accrue to local industrial production through industrial building. The latter is liable to assume fairly large dimensions; however, it is far less homogeneous in its structure and hence cannot be fitted so satisfactorily into a preconceived planning scheme.

Hence, taking a quota of 25 per cent. and 40 per cent. respectively as the direct share of industrial products in residential building, we find that expenditure on industrial requirements would be as follows:

Share of Industrial Goods in Building Investments, 1943–62
(in £ million)

Country.	Assumed Total Building Investments.		Share of Industrial Goods in Building Investments.			
			Rural (25 %).		Urban (40 %).	
	Rural.	Urban.	Total 1943–62.	Annual Average.	Total 1943–62.	Annual Average.
Egypt	162·0	161·0	40·5	2·02	64·4	3·22
Syria and Lebanon	31·5	63·0	7·9	0·40	25·2	1·26
Palestine	22·5	77·0	5·6	0·28	30·8	1·54
Turkey	178·5	168·0	44·6	2·23	67·2	3·36
Iraq	19·5	39·9	4·9	0·24	16·0	0·80
Cyprus	3·8	5·6	0·9	0·05	2·2	0·11
Transjordan	3·0	3·5	0·8	0·04	1·4	0·07
Total	420·8	518·0	105·2	5·26	207·2	10·63

Our considerations have paid no attention as yet to: (*a*) building activities for industrial purposes; (*b*) increased consumption of industrial products on the part of the urban population ; (*c*) increased use of industrial goods in farming inventory ; (*d*) the consumption of industrial products for public works (such as the construction of canals, power and irrigation plants, administrative buildings, extension of the traffic system, etc.). These items have intentionally been neglected by us in order to compensate for the share of imports in industrial goods, which will obviously continue. Forecasts present more difficulties here than in other fields, but we believe that these omissions will make up for any excess estimates. Even so we can show the following impressive picture of the potential rise in consumption goods :

ASSUMED RISE IN CONSUMPTION OF INDUSTRIAL GOODS, YEARLY AVERAGE

Country.	Consumption in					Total Rise in Consumption.
	Peasant Households.			Building.		
	No. of Persons.	Per Head.	Total.	Rural.	Urban.	
	(millions)	(£)	(£ million)	(£ million)	(£ million)	(£ million)
Egypt	13·7	5·5	75·35	2·02	3·22	80·59
Syria and Lebanon	2·5	5·5	13·75	0·40	1·26	14·41
Palestine	0·8	7·0	5·60	0·28	1·54	7·42
Turkey	14·6	5·5	80·30	2·23	3·36	85·89
Iraq	2·1	5·5	11·55	0·24	0·80	12·59
Cyprus	0·3	7·0	2·10	0·05	0·11	2·26
Transjordan	0·24	5·5	1·32	0·04	0·07	1·43
Total	34·24	—	189·97*	5·26	10·36	205·59

* The household consumption deriving from increase of population not included.

The annual increase in industrial consumption of £206 million, as demonstrated in the foregoing table, does not appear exaggerated at all and, given the presence of the factors, can safely be introduced in our calculations.

We can deal more briefly with the question of the *economic* consumptive capacity, having already discussed this point before in the chapter on agricultural development. It is a question of providing an additional purchasing power of £25 to £30 per annum and family, primarily for the agricultural population, whose increased demands are chiefly demands for industrial goods. According to our calculations this additional expenditure can easily be met from increased revenue. For a steadily growing percentage of the rural population this higher income will be achieved through their shifting to the secondary occupations, i.e. by the very process of industrialization and building referred to above. We have already drawn attention to the fact that the *per capita* income derived from industry and related fields exceeds by far that from agriculture. A transfer of workers from agriculture to industry—who, by the way, are not always required to leave their rural surroundings, as many modern industrial establishments are situated in the countryside—will, therefore, result in a considerable rise in their purchasing power.

Reverting to the peasants who will remain agricultural earners, the additional income enabling them to satisfy their desire for the better things of life—entailing in the main the supply of such goods as clothing, furniture, household utensils, medicines, books, etc.—is to be provided by raising the productivity of their work as well as by a more equal distribution of the fruit of their labour. The raising of productivity as an economic issue is largely a problem of capital investment which shall still occupy our attention. A more equitable distribution is achieved through :

(i) a reduction of the current rate of interest ;
(ii) a reduction of farm rent ;
(iii) restricting the share of intermediate trade ;
(iv) reforms in conditions of land tenure and land ownership, splitting up of the large estate and adjustment of allotments to ensure more efficient cultivation.

Most of these points are self-explanatory except, perhaps, (i) and (ii) suggesting the reduction of the rate of interest and of farm rent.

Unlike the countries of Middle and Western Europe, the Middle East only sparingly enjoys modern banking facilities, and exorbitant rates of interest continue to prevail, especially among the moneylenders to whom the peasant applies for his small amounts of credit. A rate of interest of from 30 to 50 per cent. for short-term loans, usually granted for one season, i.e. 6 to 8 months, is the established rule. Yet far higher rates of interest are by no means of rare occurrence. Even banks which would not lay themselves open to the charge of usury do not hesitate to compute a rate of interest of approximately 12 to 15 per cent. p.a. for loans issued by them (including expenses). Now it must be admitted that the absence of any political and economic security for generations has favoured the maintenance of such high rates of interest, and further, that owing to the deficient administration of justice the risk incurred by the lender in the East exceeds by far that in the West. But all this does not justify the continued application of a usurious credit system that has penetrated deeply into the Oriental economy, being tolerated by the Governments and the public alike despite the fact that laws fixing the maximum rate of interest at 9 per cent. have long been issued. Meanwhile the dispensation of justice has definitely progressed in some of these countries; besides, rates of interest have been adopted in respect of certain forms of credit, state loans and mortgage loans, which bear a close resemblance to the rates found in western countries. The claim for a government-controlled uniform reduction of the interest borne by Oriental agriculture is therefore entirely justified.

The same holds true of farm rent, which in actual fact is closely connected with the question of interest paid. A high rate of interest charged on money lent is inevitably attended with a high rate for the lease of land. The reduction of interest would go a long way towards easing the burden of cultivators, who are over head and ears in debt, more especially if followed up by a lowering of the farm rent, a measure which would be tantamount to a transfer of part of the agricultural rent from the landowner to the tenant. In Egypt, for instance, half of the cultivable land is, according to Anhoury and Minost, in the hands of the big landowners, who draw very high amounts of rent from the cultivators. The total amount of rent is estimated at about 30 million Egyptian pounds annually or about £E.10 per Feddan. A reduction by 40 per cent. would still leave a considerable amount in the hands of the landowners.

What would be the effect of the foregoing measures translated into figures? The following is only a rough calculation applied to conditions in Egypt and is, besides, based on the pre-war level of prices and of living:

	£ Million.
(*a*) Reduction of the rate of interest	3
(*b*) Lowering of farm rent in respect of 3 million Feddans . .	12
(*c*) Reduction of profits of intermediate trade through improved marketing	2
(*d*) Raising of agricultural productivity by 50 per cent. through improved cultivation and extension of cultivated area (from 90 to 135 I.U. per head of male earners, see pages 67–68) . .	39·7
In all:	56·7

As these, in part very incisive, measures cannot all be introduced simultaneously, but will have to be spread over a number of years, the result aspired to, i.e. the rise in the income of the Fellah, will also become only gradually apparent. We have further assumed that during the same period the purchasing power of the peasant will have increased by another £59 million as a result of the improvement in prices for agricultural products. An additional income of £116 million will thus accrue to the whole of the Fellah population. This means an increase that will be more than sufficient to cover the rise in expenditure of £77 million envisaged by us with regard to industrial consumption goods and rural buildings, and still leaves a sufficient margin to meet the increased cost of food.

(*b*) Our second chief question was the capacity of the local industrial production to compete with imports from abroad. Up to the present the situation has been as follows :

Until 1913 the Oriental countries used to meet the overwhelmingly greater part of their needs for industrial products from imports ; among the main exceptions were foodstuffs prepared by machinery. The war of 1914–18 led, for the same reasons as the present conflict, to an appreciable emancipation of the local markets from foreign manufacturers. This tendency continues to an increasing degree and was lately strengthened again by the difficulties in obtaining foreign supplies during wartime. Taking the example of Egypt once more, we find in the following noteworthy comparison that the country has seen a considerable decline in the import of a series of important and quantitatively considerable articles of consumption, while its own production in the same articles has simultaneously risen. Hence it is not improbable that of the pre-war £E.5½ *per capita* industrial consumption, of which £E.4 is produced locally and about £E.1·5 *per capita* is still brought from abroad, a further substantial part will be manufactured in the country.

As the table shows, the increase in the import of production goods is tremendous and a conspicuous indication of the growing productive capacity of local industry. This is corroborated by the declining import of industrial consumption goods.

Further, however, the industries, which have been tried and tested, will certainly be in a position (if the present tariff protection continues) to cover a great part of the demand which would result from any rise in the living standard of the rural and urban population, housing needs included. We therefore believe that any question regarding the competitive capacity of numerous Egyptian industries in the future may be answered in the affirmative. Naturally this calls for the continued influence of other factors besides the present tariff policy which, as

IMPORTS INTO EGYPT IN 1913 AND IN 1938 [1]

	Unit.	1913.	1938.	1938 as against 1913 in %.
Machinery and Raw Materials :				
Benzine	tons	1,884	33,250	1,765
Printing ink	kg.	42,092	231,437	550
Bars, iron or steel . . .	tons	42,764	74,709	175
Oils, mineral and lubricating	tons	9,039	126,833	1,403
Vegetable oils for industry	tons	3,368	17,371	516
Precision tools and scientific instruments	£E.	56,034	352,681	629
Motors and special machinery for various industries .	£E.	741,796	2,324,890	313
Mazout	tons	8,302	229,113	2,760
Wool yarn	kg.	162,868	292,634	180
Silk and artificial silk yarn	kg.	200,094	2,024,202	1,012
Industrial Consumption Goods :				
Matches	£E.	81,368	32,141	40
Beer	tons	7,878	6,021	76
Leather shoes	pairs	792,006	47,178	6
Cement	tons	193,987*	47,414	24
Confectionery and jams .	£E.	100,207	38,506	38
Cotton blankets and coverlets	£E.	112,212	7,145	6
Tanned leather	£E.	142,996	31,543	22
Flour of wheat, spelt and meslin	tons	203,547	3,633	2
Cotton yarn	kg.	2,693,885	772,541	29
Bedsteads, metal	£E.	81,614	1,209	2
Furniture, wood. . . .	£E.	291,112*	31,987	11
Alimentary pastes . . .	tons	806	109	14
Soap, common	tons	7,303	3,710	51
Carpets	metre	346,719	40,254	12
Tarbushes	dozen	56,565	7,133	13
Cotton piece goods . .	kg.	29,696,437	16,956,357	58
Glass and glassware . .	£E.	557,290*	251,346	45

* Average of 1924–8.

already mentioned, decidedly promotes industry. The quality of Egyptian products will have to become relatively equivalent to that of the foreign articles ; which is not yet so in every case. Similarly, the productivity of Egyptian industrial workers in a number of processing industries is still below that of the European or American worker. For the time being, these disadvantages are largely balanced by the incomparably lower

[1] M. I. Schatz, "Le Développement Industriel de l'Egypte, vu á travers les statistiques demographiques et douanières." From the special number of *Revue d'Egypte Economique et Financière*, April, 1940.

wages paid for local Oriental labour. When the latter rise, the efficiency of the operatives will have to increase as well.

In Syria and the Lebanon the situation in this respect appears somewhat more favourable, because the industrial agility of the population of that country has for decades been calling industrial enterprises into being. As a consequence, local workers there show a more favourable disposition towards intensified industrialization than those in Egypt and in the certainly far less developed Iraq and Transjordan. But in view of the very limited scope of these enterprises in the Syrian States, no definite prognosis can be offered as to the capacity of local production for competition with foreign produce, if and when the former assumes larger dimensions.

Turkey is characterized by a clear-cut policy of developing local industry at the expense of imports on a scale scarcely known elsewhere. Being the principal director of production and industry, the state has no immediate problems of foreign competition to fear.

(*c*) The Availability of Workers and Technical Staff

The general tendency towards increase of population, coupled with the shifting of workers from rural to urban occupations, will doubtless go far to satisfy the rising demand for industrial labour. According to our estimate included in the table on page 88, very substantial additions to the number of industrial earners are to be expected as a result of these trends, although the percentages themselves will show only moderate rises. Take Egypt again as example. Instead of 588,000 industrial earners in 1934–5 there would be 1,053,000 in 1962. A considerable proportion of this increase will be engaged in the production of industrial goods for the peasant population as well as for rural housing, as may be seen from the following estimate :

Let it be assumed that, according to the estimates on page 78, an additional amount of £80·6 million will be spent directly on manufactured goods in 1962, a demand will then arise for 269,000 new industrial workers, on the basis of £300 as the average value of gross output per worker. A further demand for secondary produce can, moreover, be expected to result from the building industry. According to our tables on pp. 76–7 (first line) the potential investment in housing, rural and urban, amounts to approximately £10·9 million per annum, after deducting the share of industrial goods in this total, which has been estimated by us at £5·24 million. The cost of paid labour in building has not been computed here, but may be estimated at 30 per cent. of total costs (excluding industrial goods used in construction), i.e. at £3·3 million. This amount may, on a conservative estimate, provide work for 55,000 people on an annual wages basis of £60 per earner. Altogether we shall thus have 324,000 earners in secondary occupations, building included, so that only 141,000 earners would be available to cater for the higher needs of the urban population in " secondary " products. These figures, however, provide for a reserve, as the rising degree of efficiency in industry is bound to decrease the number of workers required to produce the same unit of goods. Another reserve is provided in that part of labour which has always been drawn upon for building, and which should properly be deducted from the above figure of total potential building workers.

As to training, the great majority of such workers can easily be trained within the country itself. A certain dependence upon foreign countries will exist in a different field ; that of planning and direction of production and the processes of production. Even in the relatively autonomous new Turkish industrial development where great stress is laid on independence from any foreign influence, the foreign expert was absolutely necessary as either factory engineer, foreman, or specialist worker, to whom specific duties were entrusted or who must train the native workers. This reliance upon the experience of the West, an experience which constitutes the fruit of accumulated Western thought and knowledge, will certainly continue during the near future. It will, however, not prove a hindrance to the progress of Oriental industrialization once both parties establish their relationship in the spirit of true co-operation. The example of other Asiatic countries in the process of industrialization has shown that the training of able and skilled workers from native stock, the industrial aptitude of which has been denied for a long time, can produce operatives for many industrial working processes. Very favourable conditions have developed in Palestine where a human element possessing special qualifications for modern production processes has emerged. (Cp. also Chapter IX.)

4. Development of Transport Systems, Public Services, etc.

It is a fact corroborated by developments in all countries that an increase in the real income per head of the population is invariably associated with a rise in the demand for so-called tertiary products, i.e. for services such as are offered by transport facilities, the state and its institutions (education, health, courts, army, police, etc.), by commerce, and by the liberal professions. A higher value of turnover in production and trade entails larger amounts in respect of trade and agents' commissions. Again, a higher income from these sources allows for a larger margin of expenditure on such items as the services of doctors, teachers, and owners of hotels or establishments for recreation and amusement, etc. In distressed areas where only one physician could make a living in former times, a number of medical practitioners will then find a livelihood. The same is true of all other liberal professions and, of course, likewise of persons in the service of the state. The percentage of people following such occupations will therefore tend to rise. Indications of such a process are ample in Oriental countries. Trans-

Country.	Railway Lines (1934)		Motor Vehicles (1937) per 10,000 Persons.
	per 100 sq. kms.	per 10,000 Persons.	
	(in kms.)	(in kms.)	(in units).
European countries :			
Great Britain and N. Ireland	13·5	7·0	477
Germany	14·6	10·3	213
France	11·7	15·4	526
Switzerland	14·2	14·2	196
Belgium	33·7	12·4	244
Denmark	12·5	14·6	357
Oriental countries : *			
Egypt (total area)	0·50†	3·1	21
Syria and Lebanon	0·72	3·9	30
Palestine	2·58	5·3	62‡
Turkey	0·91	4·2	6
Iraq	0·27	3·3	19
Cyprus	1·23	1·7	61

* Figures for Oriental countries refer to the year 1938.
† If the settled area only is taken into account, the figure is 14·7.
‡ If registered vehicles are taken into account, the figure of 100 is reached.

port is an outstanding example of existent prospects. Although it has developed rapidly during the two wars, it is still far from reaching the average figures per unit of area or population attained decades ago in more advanced countries.

There is, therefore, ample room left for future progress in this field. Many new railway lines and roads, a large number of new postal services, aerial communications and shipping services are needed to achieve anything approaching the standards attained by western countries decades ago, and to cater for the increased population of Oriental lands. The same holds good as regards all other public and state services. The number of officials has grown at a rate considerably exceeding that of the population increase. But in addition to the normal expansion caused by the development of all the aforementioned activities, state initiative will produce new and enlarged services in the sphere of health, education, social insurance, etc.

In Middle Eastern countries, with their primitive agrarian structure, the proportion of those engaged in tertiary callings is between 10 and 23 per cent. of all occupations. Some of these countries have obviously remained below the percentage of 15 which Colin Clark considers as a minimum.[1] Taking this as the future minimum standard for Oriental lands, we are in a position not only to draw certain conclusions concerning the scope of additional employment within this vocational group, but also to attempt an estimate as to the general trend of earnings as well. For lack of accurate and separate statistics we shall treat the trend of the rise in earnings prevalent in secondary and tertiary occupations as practically identical.

What, then, are the direct effects of industrialization and its concomitants on the standard of living? To begin with, there is the higher remuneration of those engaged in secondary and tertiary occupations as compared with the wages or incomes of earners in agriculture; second comes the rise in productivity, and consequently in income, resulting from improvements in the production technique of modern industry as well as in transport and other services as against the primitive working methods previously employed.

It must be admitted from the outset that the calculation of these effects involves a higher degree of uncertainty than prognoses in agriculture, where part at least of the factors of production are static or fixed by nature (land, water). Even if those

[1] Colin Clark, *The Economics of 1960*, 1942.

responsible for industrial development were to be invested with full planning powers, a large margin would still prove indispensable in order to allow for the many unforeseen deviations from the envisaged course of production which are liable to occur, and which may manifest themselves either in the general programme, in the average cost of production and of materials, or the efficiency of workers and of new devices. This is particularly the case when there is no planning in the exact sense of the word, but merely a general guiding policy to that effect; then our computations cannot aim at providing more than an indication of the order of magnitude. On the other hand, in limiting our estimates to wages which constitute the net income of the employed, we can eliminate a number of doubtful factors.

On the basis of available data we assume that the average annual income of those engaged in secondary occupations was £40 in 1934–5; and further that it will rise to £70 in 1962 owing to the general trend of social improvements. These figures are the outcome of the following considerations:

Enquêtes into the conditions and earnings of artisans in Egypt revealed that the average annual income per head of those employed can be estimated at about £E.40.[1] With regard to the industrial worker the average annual *per capita* wages were found to be in the neighbourhood of £35 in Syria and £40 to £50 in Egypt. Salaries and wages earned by the overwhelming majority of officials and clerks, as well as by workers in transport and other services, are on a similar scale, the rates payable in the case of higher officials and superior personnel having no marked effect on the average in view of the limited number of earners belonging to this particular category.

As already pointed out, wage rates in industry and the services will be in accord with the general upward trend which is to be anticipated in the Middle East as a result of the adoption of an improved production technique, the insistence of labour on better wages and the rising cost of food. If, in 1934–5, the latter amounted to £20 per industrial earner, it must be expected to reach the sum of £30 by 1962. The margin left for the satisfaction of other needs will thus be £40 per earner as against the former £20.

Only in the case of Palestine, where detailed investigations are available as to the average earnings of workers engaged in

[1] Cp., for instance, A. Fournet, "L'artisanat egyptien," in *L'Egypte Contemporaine*, 1941.

industry and the services, have different figures been inserted for both 1934–5 and 1962, namely LP.60 and LP.80, respectively, for Arab workers, and LP.100 and LP130, respectively, for Jewish workers.

EARNERS IN SECONDARY AND TERTIARY OCCUPATIONS AND THEIR INCOMES[1] IN 1934–5 AND 1962

Country.	1934–5				1962					
	Number of Earners (in 1,000s).		Earned Income (in 1,000 £).		Assumed Number of Earners (in 1,000s).			Assumed Earned Income (in 1,000 £).		
	Secondary.	Tertiary.	Secondary.	Tertiary.	Secondary.	Tertiary.	Total.	Secondary.	Tertiary.	Total.
Egypt . . .	588	1,135	23,580	45,400	1,053	1,701	2,754	73,710	119,070	192,780
Turkey . .	656	785	26,240	31,400	1,680	2,160	3,840	117,600	151,200	268,800
Syria . . .	230		9,200		306	414	720	21,420	28,980	50,400
Iraq . . .	164		6,560		179	137	316	12,530	9,590	22,120
Cyprus . .	56		2,240		44	42	86	3,080	2,940	6,020
Palestine . .	1,205		16,500		435	650	1,085	52,550	76,500	129,050
thereof:										
Arabs . .	100		6,000		80	160	240	6,400	12,800	19,200
Jews . . .	105		10,500		355	490	845	46,150	63,700	109,850
Transjordan .	15		600		18	19	37	1,260	1,330	2,590
Total .	3,834		161,660		3,715	5,123	8,838	287,150	389,610	671.760

As can be seen from this table, an earned income of about £672 million is to be expected in 1962 for 8,838,000 persons employed in industries and trades, and in the services, as against £162 million in respect of 3,834,000 in 1934–5, i.e. an increase in earning capacity of £510 million. If we add to this the additional net income accruing to the agricultural population, which has been calculated by us at £360 million, we arrive at an aggregate amount of £870 million. This formidable sum gives us an idea of the huge extension in scope and the transformation in the structure of production and consumption in the Middle East which may be called out by planned development. However, the magnitude of these figures should not frighten us. If the progress made in more developed countries were to be measured in the same way, a similar multiple would emerge. Within a relatively short time the production of goods and services, and with it the national income, has doubled and trebled in those countries. Neither will it affect the present conclusions if the dates of the period chosen are changed. The

[1] The difference between the Egyptian pounds and the other pounds equal to the pound sterling (= 2½%) has been neglected in the following as well as in the foregoing tables.

span of time selected is of no material importance for the feasibility of the scheme in question. It is solely the level of prices which would have to remain in the neighbourhood of the figures quoted here.

To summarize : The prerequisite conditions for a permanent rise in the standard of living of the bulk of the Oriental masses are present as far as concerns potential increase in consumption, physical and otherwise, capacity for competition with other countries and availability of labour. This, however, does not solve the problems connected with the supply of capital. The latter have to be approached within the framework of the general planning of economic world reconstruction after the war, and are the subject of the following chapter.

CHAPTER VII

THE FINANCE OF PLANNED DEVELOPMENT

1. The Rôle of Capital in the Development of Backward Territories

Although the importance of capital supply has repeatedly been stressed in previous chapters, the subject requires to be treated at greater length, for it constitutes one of the chief problems of post-war reconstruction in the area.

The economic history of the last two hundred years has revealed the significance of capital investment for the opening up of undeveloped countries. The task of providing capital has now become the fundamental element of all development plans for such countries. To-day we know that the wealth of society should be measured not in gold, jewels or consumption goods but in productive equipment; and that these means of production themselves derive in turn from the ever-improving manufacture of goods. The wealth and progress of a country depend first and foremost on the scope and variety of " capital goods " available for new production.

Even when a territory is adequately provided with unexploited mineral resources and sufficient workers, it is not in a position to advance beyond a moderate degree of well-being unless capital is introduced in the form of means of production. The investment of capital in the form of power machinery, plant for extracting mineral resources, transport routes and means of transport, technical, chemical and physical laboratories, knowledge of experts and countless machines for the manufacture of the variegated series of human requirements—all these together make it possible to utilize the latent possibilities of human society in order to produce prosperity and wealth, or overcome poverty. A higher level of productivity, that is, an increase in income as well as more plentiful employment of those members of the society who are capable of work, cannot be achieved without a constant and large-scale investment of such productive goods.

Hence capital constitutes the most important material element for achieving and increasing prosperity at the disposal of the human will to progress. But the employment of such productive capital or capital goods requires the availability of the necessary money capital, that is, the financial means.[1]

Where, in the absence of the prerequisite natural or social conditions, it is impossible to provide such capital from local sources, material progress will depend upon the necessary capital being made available from external quarters, either in the form of loan capital or as a permanent transfer of capital resources ; as for example through immigrants. This relatively simple nexus, which is not always quite obvious in countries with large local accumulation of capital, can be seen even by superficial inspection under the simple conditions of undeveloped countries. Thus the efforts and hard work of a poor Fellah or native in the traditional type of farm to be found in the African or Asiatic agricultural zones produce only a fraction of the yield that can be achieved given a suitable investment of capital, either in developed countries or even in the same overseas territories. A small investment is frequently quite enough to raise the yield considerably. Similarly, higher returns are produced by the outlay of capital on the improvement and establishment of transit channels for passenger and goods traffic, and even capital spent on housing or on improvements in the field of education and hygiene will show returns in the form of increased efficiency and working capacity.

In Chapter V the differences in the figures of the agricultural output per earner of the various countries were pointed out and accounted for. An analogous explanation can be given for the different levels found in craft and industrial manufacturing. Here as well the employment of implements and machinery, which are only other forms of capital, can multiply the yield many times over. New investigations into the relation between income and investment of capital have proved, in an instructive fashion, that a rising income usually postulates a rise in capital investment per person employed. The higher the amount of capital invested per person employed, the greater are the prospects of a higher income, whether in agriculture, in industry, or in transport and other services. The table on page 92 demonstrates this relationship in a number of countries.

In trying to obtain figures for capital investment in Oriental countries, we are again confronted with the difficulties inherent in the present state of statistics in these regions. But as far as

[1] The difference between money capital and productive capital has not been dwelt upon as being irrelevant to the main issue under discussion.

the admittedly very defective data are available, similar tendencies can be traced in the territories of the Middle East as well.

CAPITAL, EXCLUDING LAND AND NATIONAL DEBTS[1]
(calculated in I.U. per head of the working population, 1913)

Country.	Buildings.	Railways.	Farm Capital.	Commercial Capital, i.e. Balance not Included in Previous Headings.	Total.	Real Income per Head of Work. Pop. per 48-hour Week.
U.S.A. .	2,480	760	360	1,560	5,160	1,191
Canada . .	1,780	655	525	1,630	4,590	1,061
Australia .	2,270	435	430	965	4,100	742
Argentine .	1,440	710	350	2,180	4,680	(800)
Germany .	—	410	—	—	3,130	704
France . .	1,120	—	175	—	3,060	629
Britain . .	1,335	460	137	1,658	3,590	966
Italy . . .	460	—	120	—	1,430	328
Spain . .	485	—	160	—	1,435	408
Spain, 1930	—	—	—	—	2,150	600
Austria . .	410	295	—	—	1,580	452
Hungary. .	310	215	—	—	1,110	220
Sweden . .	880	170	190	1,440	2,680	474
Belgium . .	550	—	—	—	2,190	470
Japan . .	160	51	—	—	460	128
Japan, 1930.	360	57	—	—	980	301

As a result of the conspicuous interest in the economic life of Egypt which foreign capital has shown during recent generations, certain figures exist in that country relative to the amounts invested in railways, farms and irrigation, building, etc. This material has made it possible to compute the data summarized below :

CAPITAL INVESTMENTS IN EGYPT, EXCLUDING LAND
(Estimates for 1937)

	Buildings.	Farms.	Railways.	Irrigation, etc.	Industry and Commerce.	Total.
In £E. million .	186	116	31	37	180	550
In £E. per head of the working population . .	30·5	19	5	6	29·5	90
In I.U. (approx. figures) . . .	152	95	25	30	147	450

[1] Colin Clark, *The Conditions of Economic Progress*, p. 389.

Comparing the figures for Egypt with those of other countries as reproduced in the preceding table, we see again and in a very striking way how the picture of a wide gap between the standards of Western countries and of undeveloped areas repeats itself in the case of capital investment. Average investment in building per earner is trifling compared to the figures for the countries of America and Western Europe. Only Japan, in 1913, approaches these low figures, probably on account of the simple structure of the majority of Japanese buildings. The more solid urban buildings in that country are so few in number that they could not raise the average. Figures for Industry, Commerce and for Farm Capital, even adding the expenditure for irrigation, likewise remain far behind the corresponding data for the countries first mentioned. The total figure of 450 I.U. in respect of capital investment per head in Egypt therefore represents only a fraction of the totals of other countries indicated in the table—Japan 1913 again excluded—and thus discloses in unmistakable form an exceedingly low level of average investment as compared with the average capital equipment of more progressive zones.

There are no complete statistics for other Oriental countries, Palestine excepted. But for investments in Railways fairly complete data are available, and are included in the table below.

EXPENDITURE ON RAILWAYS

Country.	Railway Lines 1938/39 (in km.).	Expenditure per km. (in 1,000 £).	Total Expenditure (in 1,000 £).	No. of Earners 1939 (in 1,000s).	Capital Expenditure per Head (£).	Capital Expenditure per Head (I.U.).
Turkey .	7,071	9·0	63,639	8,458	7·5	37
Egypt . .	5,019*	8·0†	30,952	6,338	4·9	25
Palestine	647‡	8·0	5,176	496	10·4	52
Syria . .	1,099	6·5	7,143	1,050	6·8	34
Iraq . .	1,304	7·3	9,519	925	10·3	51

* *Thereof*: State lines—3,604 km.;
Private lines—1,415 km.

† This figure represents state expenditure; private expenditure amounts to £1,500 per km. (Private railways.)

‡ Including 203 km. Sinai—Kantara—Raffa.

In this particular branch of capital investment the picture of a rather early stage of development is again encountered. As to other branches, it appears that the figures for Egypt can on the whole be regarded as representative for the standard capital equipment of Oriental lands. These figures seem, moreover, to represent high levels, for other countries have attracted far less foreign capital than has Egypt, the Oriental land famous for the relatively large investments in agriculture, irrigation and commerce.

In any case, the differences between the average capital investments of the various countries appear to be negligible in view of the great similarity in the size of capital equipment in Fellahin agriculture and the conspicuous absence of any large-scale industrial enterprises as compared with their occurrence in the West. Palestine, thanks to the presence of a well-developed progressive sector, seems to be an exception. As demonstrated in the table below, figures here approach those of the advanced countries in Europe.

CAPITAL INVESTMENT IN THE JEWISH SECTOR OF PALESTINE EXCLUDING LAND, COMMUNICATIONS AND BANK DEPOSITS 1921–40

	Building.*	Farm.	Industry.	Commercial.	Total.
Total in million LP.	42·3	14·6	12	9·2	78·1
Per head of the working population in LP.	201	69	57	43	370
In International Units per Head :					
Jewish Palestine (1921–40) (approx. figures)	1,005	345	285	215	1,850
Egypt (1937)	152	125†	147		424
Great Britain (1913)	1,335	137	1,658		3,130

* Including industrial and farm building.
† Including irrigation works (30 I.U. per head).

The large increase of capital investment in Palestine led to a rise in the *per capita* gross yield of the employed, and therewith increased the net return as well. It should, however, be borne in mind that comparisons over different periods are liable to be affected through alterations in the value of money in the interim. Unfortunately, figures are too scanty to allow for computations to be made in respect of other Oriental countries. Yet these would, no doubt, show a similar line of development to that which characterized the capitalist production of the Western countries, notwithstanding all variations deriving from the difference in conditions, natural and political, in the East and West.

2. The Distribution of Capital Investment in the Past in the Opening-up of Oriental Countries

In the past the problem of financing economic development in Oriental countries had three aspects. First, local capital accumulation was limited, so that large-scale development projects requiring considerable capital could, as a rule, not be undertaken from inland resources. Second, the Oriental capitalist was, even as far as his resources were available, not prepared to invest his money anonymously, so to speak, i.e. in limited liability companies, which is the normal form of such development enterprises. Finally, the conditions current in the Ottoman Empire were not regarded by foreign capitalists as adequate for the security of ownership and property, so that specific institutions of a political and economic character were developed and used in order to safeguard the investment and further the interests connected therewith.

The low yield of the soil and of industry, particularly in view of the extensive official interference with income and property, left the local producers scarcely more than the barest minimum necessary for their existence. Hence in Oriental countries it was impossible for capital to accumulate in any measure that could even tend to cover local requirements for purposes of development. Orientals were disinclined to make investments involving any greater risks than are found in house and landed property and the purchase of jewellery.

Foreign capitalists, on the other hand, who were familiar with the modern methods of employing capital customary in Western Europe and the U.S.A., demanded as a prerequisite for the employment of their capital the provision of rights which were frequently used as means to attain political ends, and which hence stood in the way of genuine economic and social development. In addition, the financial terms for the investment of foreign capital in Oriental countries were often imposed through outside pressure and were thus not determined on the basis of free agreement.

This in turn had a dubious effect on the productivization of Oriental countries. The capital influx, in view of its scope, might have led to a broader development, benefiting the whole of the population. As things were, however, accompanying political conditions or auxiliary objectives not infrequently rendered the original economic aims of no avail or restricted them to limited spheres only.

The following review of the employment of foreign capital in Oriental countries shows the consequence of this. First and foremost, transport undertakings were financed because they were calculated to promote and cheapen the distribution of foreign goods. Then followed enterprises, which themselves either manufactured or promoted the manufacture of goods intended for foreign countries—such as mining plants or banks—or else were clearly free from economic risks, on account of the nature of the product; as, for example, public utilities and water works, gas works, government companies, etc.

The foreign capital active in Turkey after the signing of the Treaty of Lausanne was invested as follows:[1]

	£ (in 1,000s).	Percentage.
Railways	39,133	61·71
Banks	10,210	16·10
Mining	3,088	4·81
Municipal concessions	4,943	7·86
Industrial enterprises	2,447	3·86
Commercial establishments	3,593	5·66
In all:	63,414	100

PAID-UP CAPITAL AND DEBENTURES OF COMPANIES OPERATING PREPONDERANTLY WITH FOREIGN CAPITAL[2]

Branches.	1914. Total.	1914. Foreign Capital.	1914. Local Capital.	1933. Total.	1933. Foreign Capital.	1933. Local Capital.
	in 1,000 £E.					
Mortgage companies	54,569	54,569	—	45,310	44,310	1,000
Banks and financial institutions	5,727	5,552	175	6,164	5,085	1,079
Agricultural and urban land	18,573	12,332	6,241	12,361	6,745	5,616
Transport and canals (excl. Suez Canal)	6,076	5,733	343	5,164	4,445	719
Industry, mining and commerce	15,357	13,405	1,952	27,242	20,780	6,462
Total	100,302	91,591	8,711	96,241	81,395	14,876

[1] *La Turquie Contemporaine*, Ankara, 1935, p. 208.

[2] A. E. Crouchley, *The Investment of Foreign Capital in Egyptian Companies and Public Debt*, 1936, p. 93. The amounts in the table comprise only part of the foreign investments in Egypt.

The classification of foreign capital in Egypt, as far as it constitutes investments in limited companies, shows a similar preference for the most secure types of investments.

But in spite of the conspicuous rôle of foreign capital, its scope was not sufficient to develop the economic resources of Oriental countries to the degree found in the mature economies of the West. Except for the aforementioned domains of investment favoured by foreign capital, the general level of capital investment, measured per head of the working population, was exceedingly low as compared with Western countries. Moreover, the preference shown by foreign capital for particular forms of investment in Oriental territories as well as the tendency of foreign investors to insist on security of ownership and property, brought about a stagnation in other spheres of economic activity, which were more important to the welfare of the country as a whole. Thus, the process of industrialization was hampered, and the human and material capacities of the local population could not be fully developed.

3. The Rôle of Capital in the Opening-up of Oriental Countries in the Future

The foregoing leads to the following conclusions regarding the part to be played by capital in the development of backward Oriental territories :

As before, Oriental countries, with the sole exception of limited zones, notably the urban ones, still constitute areas of exceedingly small capital formation from their own resources. However, if the world-wide tendencies towards improved standards of living are to assume any concrete shape among the Oriental peoples, comprehensive measures must be adopted in order to assure a steady capital supply. Such a programme demands a very considerable capital import into these territories, which will need to be directed into all economically essential fields. Local agriculture in particular, which must be regarded as singularly backward, technically and economically, will have to be given the benefit of capital investment in a far greater measure than ever before. But industrial production and transport will also stand in need of extensive capital investments in order to reach the standards of more developed industrial countries.

In consideration of the tendency to discourage the forms of foreign investment formerly prevalent in certain Oriental countries, how is the capital needed for financing new agricultural and industrial production to be provided? [1] In other words, whence will the means come which are required both for long-term investments and current short-term credits? The reply will to a large extent depend on the general principles governing reconstruction after the war. It must be taken for granted that undeveloped countries commanding such large and cheap resources of labour as do Oriental states, will be fully eligible for a generous grant of international credits in the form of capital goods and means of production; provided that they can prove their ability to pay along the lines indicated by the sponsors of the reconstruction movements in the western world. An instructive example of the approach of important American circles is a proposal made by Mr. M. Feis, one of the officials of the American State Department, in the January, 1942, issue of *Foreign Affairs*. The author treats the problem preponderantly from the viewpoint of American interests, but there seems no reason why other powers should not adopt his approach too. Mr. Feis suggests that "at the beginning of each year the American Government set aside, in the Federal Reserve Bank (or some other institution), a designated sum of dollars which would be made available to foreign nations for external payment of goods, services or debts. This sum might at the beginning be, say, three or four billions of dollars. This is designated as a rough estimate of the minimum urgent future needs of foreign countries for dollars for these purposes; but it might well have variable limits. By a process of negotiation—in which past record and current analysis would establish the limits that were reasonable—the various parts of this total sum could then be allocated for the use of particular nations. The purposes for which the allocated sums were to be available, as well as various other details of their use, such as the fractions which might be drawn upon by governments and for what purposes, could also be settled by negotiation. . . . To the extent that each foreign country drew upon the dollars allocated for its use, it would be obligated to set aside an equivalent amount in its own currency

[1] Cf. E. Monroe, *The Mediterranean in Politics*, p. 33: "For there is every indication that independent Egypt will extend nationalist principles to the business transacted on her soil, that she will subject the foreigner to unwelcome pressure and hope to retain his money while banishing his presence and his influence."

In modern Turkey, investments still owned by foreigners are subjected to stringent Government supervision, and there is no private capital from abroad forthcoming as before.

(or of other currencies, as might be agreed) available for expenditure by the United States at a designated rate of exchange. The foreign currencies so accruing to the American account would be on sale by the Federal Reserve Bank to private interests. Here also, again presumably within variable limits, the purposes for which they could be employed would be specified. There necessarily would be substantial variations in the terms of different agreements to accord with the different positions of the countries concerned—as there are, for example, in the Lend-Lease agreements under negotiation with the other American republics.

"No permanent debt would come into existence. If at the end of a specified period (say, each two years) foreign countries had not yet drawn fully upon the fund of dollars allocated, the unused remainder would be cancelled. If, on the other hand, uses had not been found for the amounts of other currencies accruing to the account of the United States, these should also be cancelled. The arrangement could be so framed as to permit use of the allocated funds within agreed limits, by private individuals for investment in the other country, or for loans to private individuals within the other country."

It is not absolutely necessary that the procedure of capital allocations for the development of backward countries should follow the scheme proposed by Mr. Feis in every respect; but it is important for an essential share of the capital needs of Oriental zones to be covered along such lines.

Yet apart from international resources, the economy of the various territories will also be required to raise means within their boundaries, if their reconstruction schemes are to be carried out effectively and according to programme. Egypt is a case in point. Although the abolition of the capitulations and the growing dislike of foreigners have reduced the former chances of profit for foreign capital, the principal and interest gained by it in that country are still quite considerable. However, the second World War has stimulated production and the accumulation of capital within the country to a hitherto unknown degree. Hence there can be no doubt that a more rigid system of taxation analogous to that adopted in more advanced countries would yield an annual public revenue large enough to afford the repayment of considerable loans for development purposes.

According to Cleland, there were, in 1936, 232,000 people in Egypt with an average annual income amounting to £420 and a total income of £97,440,000.[1] Hitherto the Exchequer's revenue from these incomes has been trifling, and even the recent income tax legislation has not altered the situation fundamentally. An increase in the rate of taxation by 20 per cent., while keeping the rate still far below that applied to the same income class in other countries, would easily result in an additional revenue of several million pounds. This is a fair sum when regarded as a source for securing the repayment of a state loan. In addition, the Egyptian Government can draw upon its Reserve Fund, which has hardly been used so far and could now serve to facilitate the financing of long-term reconstruction projects.

These measures, though in part fairly vigorous, offer the best security against the dangers involved in keeping millions of people in a state of continued distress. War prosperity will not prevent the newly acquired riches from disappearing very quickly, unless there is a definite policy of maintaining production and consumption at a satisfactory level after the war as well. The fact that there have as yet been no disturbances in that country does not preclude their occurrence at some future date. Under a changed political constellation Egypt, too, might become the scene of grave events attended with great risks for property; a development the prevention of which would render the payment of an adequate premium worth while for the capitalist class.

The most important practical issue arising from this as far as concerns the economic policy of these countries and the international bodies engaged on these tasks, would appear to be the planning of the capital investment, i.e. the proper direction of the flow of capital so as to ensure its greatest possible effectiveness for the economy as a whole.

It is evident that the realization of such a tremendous scheme must be spread over a number of years; it must be carried out step by step, and based on plans to be drawn up separately for each of the countries concerned, in conformity with the specific conditions prevailing in them.

[1] The above figures, which are taken from W. Cleland, *The Population Problem of Egypt*, refer to peace-time only. Meanwhile these figures have grown very considerably owing to war-time conditions which have led to an unprecedented increase in the profits and income of the well-to-do. However, to remain on the safe side, the old figures have been retained here.

4. Planned Capital Investment in Agriculture

In the foregoing we have demonstrated that the development of primitive agriculture, that is the raising of its productivity, is contingent primarily on the provision of new capital. An increase in agricultural productivity is brought about through a switching over to rationalized irrigation in zones of dry farming, as well as scattered irrigation and a variety of other measures such as the more extensive use of fertilisers, improved seeds, effective pest control and prevention of plant and animal diseases, proper nursing of trees, application of the selective principle in stock-breeding, more rational organization of farming (choice of sowing time, improved crop rotation, employment of improved agricultural implements and machinery) ; in short, it will be necessary to stock each farm unit with means of production, the extent of which is largely a function of the capital available per farm unit.

In this connection the size of the individual farm is not of decisive importance. Far more significant is the extent of investments per head of the rural worker. Countries with a high *per capita* investment in agriculture show an advanced level in rural life. In the same way it appears from farm accounts that the largest surpluses were realized, irrespective of the size of the individual farm, in cases showing the relatively highest capital investment per head of those engaged in agriculture.[1]

These general facts established, an attempt will be made :

(*a*) to form an idea of the total capital investments in agriculture needed by the Oriental countries ; and

(*b*) to ascertain how the requisite funds should be invested in the rural establishments which are in need of capital.

A calculation of the total investments necessary for the Oriental countries has to contend with the difficulty that conditions in these lands are not uniform. Not only do the numbers of workers per farm differ, but in addition fundamental divergencies can be observed in the elements of farming, such as irrigation farming and dry-farming, plantations and grain-growing, highly porous limestone soil and heavy loams, hilly country and plain, etc. All these call for a diversity in the investment structure. Notwithstanding this, an attempt will be made within this general framework to assess the magnitude of the sums involved by using the data which have been elaborated in connection with similar issues.

[1] D. Warriner, *Economics of Peasant Farming*, 1939, p. 4.

In Palestine, the needs of the European settlers have rendered necessary the establishment of farm types yielding higher returns corresponding to their higher standard of living. This has led to large-scale attempts to develop agricultural systems with a structure of income and expenditure analogous to that of the West. The main difference between this type and that encountered in local agriculture is naturally found in the capital equipment of these farms—apart from the different training, education and working methods of the farmers themselves. The various forms of capital equipment have repeatedly been calculated for Palestine, notably by Volcani, and range from £70 in respect of an old-type Fellah farm (house, stable, cattle, ass and implements) to £400 for a Europeanized type of local farm.

Compared with the capital value of Arab farms in Palestine and other Oriental countries, which ranges between £40 and £100, modernized Fellah farms require an additional capital outlay of at least £150 to £200. Now it cannot be expected that the great difference in capital value as between an improved type of farm and a Fellah holding is liable to be adjusted through new investments within a limited period. But if such investments are distributed over a number of years in accordance with a well-conceived plan, each country should be able to carry out schemes of rural development corresponding to the needs of the various zones within its territory. The allocation of the means would have to be undertaken and controlled by development institutions especially set up for this purpose. Any calculation of capital outlay envisaged for a future period of at least twenty years contains of necessity an element of uncertainty. Whatever the minor modifications to be introduced, an additional amount of from £150 to £200 per farm unit (Fellah holding) would decisively transform this type of Oriental economy. With this in mind, we arrive, on the basis of the figures quoted on page 68, at a capital requirement for the period up to the end of 1962 of £1,361 million, or an average annual amount of about £70 million. This amount has been computed as follows :

Number of Holdings (one holding corresponds to 1·5 male earners)

	in 1,000s.		£ million.
1962	7,535		
1934–5	5,525		
Additional holdings	2,010	each at £265 =	532·6
Existing holdings	5,525	" " £150 =	828·7
		In all :	1,361·3

This sum would have to be spent on improvement of farm installation and equipment, on working tools, stable premises, improved cattle-breeding and poultry-raising, on irrigation implements, etc.

It appears that, with the exception of Palestine, little material has been elaborated which could serve as basis for determining the financial and other needs involved in a large-scale reform of Fellahin farming. In Palestine, Mr. Volcani has studied these questions for years, and has supplied the following particulars concerning the financial requirements of various types of improved farms (see Tables on next page).

Although these figures refer to conditions in Palestine, they are nevertheless apt to illustrate the amounts needed to carry out a scheme of agricultural development in other Oriental countries as well. To furnish a detailed programme of agricultural reconstruction in respect of each of the Middle Eastern countries and zones would exceed the scope of this book. Those, however, who are sceptical as to the possibilities of far-reaching improvements are reminded that promising beginnings of such a development already exist in some of the Oriental countries.

The agricultural achievements of the new settlements established in Palestine in accordance with modern scientific precepts cannot, it is true, be easily reached in the old-type farms. Nevertheless, a number of important innovations could profitably be applied in the native farms as well. For example : local wheat varieties, grown since time immemorial, yield meagre crops and flour of poor baking quality ; the introduction of a more productive and better quality soft wheat would, therefore, mean a distinct advance. Experiments conducted by the Jewish Agency Experimental Station at Rehoboth and by the Government Agricultural Station at Acre have provided promising results, and "Morocco" seeds of soft wheat introduced from Australia into Tunis are now widely used in Jewish settlements. According to Dr. Menko Plaut, Head of the Seed-Breeding Division of the Rehoboth Station, about a third of the total wheat area in the Jewish settlements (20,000 to 25,000 dunams of a total of 70,000 to 80,000 dunams) was cultivated under soft wheat types in 1941–2. The results already available from the two preceding seasons, 1939–40 and 1940–1, have been carefully collated and cross-checked by the Rehoboth Experimental Station and the Farmers' Association. In every case the conclusion has been that soft wheat varieties provide much larger yields than the

INVESTMENT REQUIRED FOR THE EQUIPMENT OF VARIOUS TYPES OF MIXED FARMS [1]

(*A*) *Investments in the Ordinary Fellah Farm*—		
(1) Buildings:	LP.	LP.
Family dwelling, dairy and poultry buildings	30	
Hay loft	5	35
(2) Livestock:		
3 oxen	15	
2 cows	10	
1 donkey	3	
Miscellaneous	2	30
(3) Tools and Implements:		
1 plough	1	
1 threshing board	1	
Miscellaneous	3	5
Total	LP.	70
(*B*) *Investments required by the Improved Fellah Farm*—		
(1) Buildings:	LP.	LP.
Family dwelling, dairy and poultry buildings	60	
Hay loft and fence	15	75
(2) Water Installation		100
(3) Livestock:		
2 cows	25	
1 mule	15	
100 fowls	15	55
(4) Plough and Threshing Board		5
(5) Plantation		30
Total	LP.	265
(*C*) *Investments required by the Mixed Farm in Transition Stage* (*Europeanized*)—		
(1) Buildings:	LP.	LP.
Family dwelling (one room, kitchen and veranda)	80	
Dairy barn and poultry house	60	
Fence and farmyards	15	155.
(2) Water Installation:		
Pump house and central pipes (4″)	100	
Portable sprinkler	40	140
(3) Livestock:		
1 cow.	40	
25 fowls at 150 mils	3·750	
5 beehives	5	
Miscellaneous	1·250	50
(4) Tools and Implements		10
(5) Plantation		45
Total	LP.	400

native wheat grown on the same soils and under the same methods of cultivation. In fact the "Morocco" and Australian varieties have been found to provide far higher yields than native types. For instance during 1940–1, the "Morocco 386" sown in Afikim, Hefziba, Merhavia, etc., provided an average yield

[1] J. Eleazari-Volcani, *Planned Mixed Farming*, 1938, pp. 136–7.

of 187·1 kgs. per dunam as compared with 123·8 kgs. of native wheat. The Australian "CCC", cultivated at Ain Harod, Bet Alfa and elsewhere, provided an average yield of 170·1 kgs. per dunam as against 117·4 kgs. of the native type wheat. "BIPM" seeds grown in Ain Harod, Tel Joseph and also far south in Negba, etc., produced on the average 159·7 kgs. per dunam as compared with 107·8 kgs. from local types. In some places these varieties yielded more than 300 kgs. per dunam. Although a doubling of yields may not always be expected, it seems certain that at least a one-third increase may be generally reckoned upon when soft wheat seeds are used.[1] Thus an important improvement like this obviously requires no more than the supply of proper seeds and Fellahin instruction in their use.

Agrarian conditions in Syria and the Lebanon closely resemble those of Palestine. Hence figures regarded as adequate for developing Fellahin farming in Palestine can rightfully be taken as a point of departure for similar calculations referring to agriculture in Syria. In one respect, however, there exists a striking difference in the potential resources of Palestine and of its northern neighbour. The water resources of Syria and the Lebanon greatly exceed those of Palestine, and, despite many analogous features as to methods of cultivation and exploitation of soil, irrigated agriculture offers wider possibilities in Syria. Both the area of irrigable lands and the amount of water available from rivers, lakes and ground water are far larger there than in Palestine. Besides, many of the valuable devices evolved in Palestine for lifting ground water by motor pumps have so far been applied in Syria on a limited scale only. All competent observers of the situation there are at one in stressing the tremendous possibilities of irrigated cultures in Syria and their importance for increasing productivity and raising the standard of living. Again, the central problem is one of capital supply needed to finance the necessary investments in hydraulic works, for which plans were, in some instances, ready long ago and, in others, can easily be drawn up in accordance with local experience and on the model of the well-developed irrigation technique of Palestine.

In Egypt a very important factor in raising the productivity of local farming appears to be the introduction of improved dairy cattle. An interesting booklet issued by the Agricultural

[1] *Palestine and Middle East*, 1941, No. 12.

Department of Assiut College reports on the fundamental fact that the local cows have neither the temperament nor the capacity for high milk production. Attempts were made to remedy the position by the import of highly improved foreign stock. The experiment so far has shown promising results, from several points of view. Besides the rise in the formerly very scanty milk output, a diversification of farming is to be expected. For her cash income Egypt depends almost exclusively upon cotton and cotton by-products. This one crop accounts for 95 per cent. of her exports. Yet cotton is an extremely speculative crop—to some extent in yield but particularly in price. When the price is low there is universal want—no money except for the barest necessities.

Not only from the immediate economic viewpoint but also from the more general consideration of the maintenance of soil fertility, such exclusive reliance upon this single crop is unfortunate. Cotton leaves in the soil little residue of organic matter, without which even the most fertile soils become unproductive. This loss of soil fertility is especially rapid in the perennially irrigated soil of Egypt which now receives practically no Nile sediment and yet is expected to produce two or three crops per year. Egypt greatly needs a " cash crop " supplementary to cotton and favourable to the maintenance of soil fertility. Apart from the increased production of milk, which is also of great importance from the commercial and nutritional standpoint, dairy farming yields organic manure, a vital necessity for the soil under the conditions prevailing in Egypt. Provided cattle of high productive capacity can be secured, a commercial dairy industry should go far towards meeting these basic needs. Experiments of the Assiut Agricultural Department have proved that the milk output of the pure-bred Jersey cow is about three times that of the native Egyptian cow, and that a half-Jersey still yields twice as much as her native Egyptian mother or half-sister.

The pamphlet in question closes with the following remarks :

> In fact the fundamental purpose of the whole project demands that it be self-supporting in order to demonstrate in practice that with high producing animals to utilize the clover and maize crops, which produce so bountifully in Egypt, dairying could become a worthy supplementary crop to cotton and could be depended upon to maintain the fertility of the soil. With this more secure economic foundation a rise in general social standards would become more possible ; children could be better clothed, fed and schooled ; uplifting moral and spiritual forces more readily stimulated.

Another instructive example of the improved prospects of agriculture, given by even relatively small capital investments, is offered by the experience collected in a Balkan country in respect of poultry farming.

Throughout South-Eastern Europe, poultry husbandry is of a very primitive nature. Poor methods of breeding, feeding, and housing and high incidence of disease prevail. The birds run wild throughout the village and, except in winter, must pick up most of their own feed. Winter feeding usually consists of sporadically throwing a little grain to them. In general no poultry house of any sort is provided, and the birds roost in trees, fences or other convenient objects even during the winter season, which is severe in most parts of the region. Tuberculosis, bacillary white diarrhœa and other diseases are uncontrolled and spread easily because of the conditions under which the birds are kept and the lack of trained veterinarians or poultry technicians. The average egg production per bird per year is about 65 to 75 eggs; the poultry are so scrawny as to be of little value for food, and the average flock is only 12 to 15 in number. Nevertheless this small, inefficient enterprise provides an important share of the small cash income of the average peasant family. Eggs must be sold in order to purchase salt, matches, kerosene, and the few other essential purchases of the peasant household, and hence few are retained at home.

In view of this depressing state of affairs a long-term programme of poultry improvement was inaugurated in Bulgaria, including the introduction of American breeding stock, establishment of modernized poultry houses, improvement of feeding, hatching of eggs with incubators, systematic disease prevention, etc. The following quotation shows the effect of these measures in the village selected as a Centre for the application and demonstration of the new method of poultry farming:

> Only pure-bred Rhode Island Reds are now kept in the village and the average egg production per bird has risen to 125 eggs annually. An average profit of $1 per bird is now secured in the village, and a flock of 50 pullets will thus double the previous cash income of about $50 per farm per year. The village now supplies chicks and breeding stock to a large part of the county, and two other villages in the county serve the remaining rural communities. The standard of living in this first village has greatly improved as a result of the desire of the peasant population to develop similar programmes for other agricultural enterprises and translate the increased income into higher standards of

> nutrition, health, sanitation, and recreation. The village now employs a *homemaking* specialist and a public health nurse and shares a doctor and a veterinary surgeon with nearby villages. During the summer a kindergarten is operated. The village has become a demonstration of rural improvement for Bulgaria and has been visited by people from other Balkan and Middle Eastern Countries.[1]

Hence here, too, a limited capital investment has sufficed to change the living conditions of the peasants to a considerable degree.

5. Planned Capital Investment in Industry

In an outline of capital requirements for future industrial development it is impossible to give more than general indications as to the sums needed for industrial expansion. In view of the diversified and in a way individual character of the latter, any attempt at an accurate calculation of the total capital outlay on a country-wide scale seems questionable. Only by investigating the prospects of the various industrial branches for each area separately could we arrive at any definite figure. For the time being, however, we content ourselves with a general formula, on the assumption that, given a certain number of industrial earners as introduced in preceding tables, the capital required to establish the industries employing them will constitute the product of the number of workers multiplied by the average investment. In our case it would mean that the industrialization of Oriental countries involves a capital outlay of between £743 and £1,486 million, distributed over two decades, or an annual allocation of about £37 to £74 million. In view of the sums invested annually by smaller countries, it seems possible to introduce amounts of this order of magnitude in a long-view development scheme for countries still in the first stages of industrialization.

The capital needed for industrial development is not likely to be raised in the same manner as that for agriculture. Local capitalists are familiar with conditions in agriculture, a sphere in which the first large investments were made in capital works with a view to increasing production in certain commercial plantations. In the industrial field, however, the situation is different. The class of well-to-do entrepreneurs, the backbone

[1] Clayton E. Whipple, "Poultry Improvement in South-eastern Europe", in *Foreign Agriculture*, 1942, Vol. 6, No. 11 (a Monthly issued by the U.S.A. Department of Agriculture in Washington, D.C.).

of the process of industrialization in Western countries, has not appeared in the Orient to any considerable extent for reasons which cannot be gone into here. Modern Oriental Governments have tried to cope with the resultant situation by mobilizing considerable sums out of their budgets for the financing of the new industrial production. Turkey and Iran were the first to do so; and in some measure Egypt and Iraq followed the same policy for certain sectors of industrial life. There are good reasons for assuming that this state of affairs will have to persist. The local formation of capital is not yet sufficient to provide all the means needed. Yet when it undertakes a comprehensive industrialization scheme, even a generous state can finance no more than part thereof. In addition, saving in Oriental countries is still far behind Western standards, which explains why it is so difficult for Eastern economies to catch up with the West. The chairman of the Egyptian Industrialists' Association has expressed himself as follows on this point: "The greatest difficulty in the development of Egyptian industry is the lack of the necessary capital and of experts. I should neglect my duty towards this country and its youth were I not to stress the necessity for receiving precisely the help which we need and which is offered without any ulterior motive."[1]

Such descriptions as the foregoing do not apply to Egypt alone. Countries like Turkey, Iraq and Iran cannot raise the capital necessary for their industrialization exclusively from the state resources of the country, whether these be taxation or public funds in the form of state credits. Hence there is no other way, as already pointed out by us, than the *international* supply of funds for the development of the backward areas. What we could demonstrate for agriculture and industry holds good no less for public works and transport. In all these spheres, local and international sources of capital must combine to effect a satisfaction of the need for capital.

In order to form an idea of how the huge amounts needed can be secured, an attempt will be made to compare the total capital investment required with the sums likely to be obtained. As a result of our calculations we have arrived at a total capital outlay of £2,476 million in respect of investments in industry and agriculture during the whole of the planning period envisaged

[1] The above passage clearly refers to conflicting opinions regarding foreign capital investment in Egypt which has recently been the subject of lively discussion in financial quarters. Cp. *L'Egypte Industrielle*, No. 8, April 15, 1939, p. 30.

in this book. The yearly average would thus approximate to £123 million, a figure which may serve as an indication of the actual investment needs, although these will, in the nature of things, be considerably smaller during the first years of the planning period and reach their peak towards its end. Now, how are these annual £123 millions to be raised? As set out in the first part of the present chapter, a substantial proportion of the financial needs will have to be met from annual allocations to be provided by the great international reconstruction agencies. These allocations should, for all the countries of the Middle Eastern zone, average £45 million a year, it being again understood that these amounts would be smaller at the beginning of the planning period in question and show a progressive increase as time goes on. The annual capital requirements being estimated at £123 million, another £78 million would require to be raised from their own resources by the countries concerned. In view of the growing development and opening up of these vast regions, an amount of £78 million does not seem exaggerated. Measured in terms of net earned income and net output in industry and agriculture this amount represents no more than 6½ per cent. of the total sums arrived at in the foregoing calculations, a percentage that could and should be derived from saving part of the income.

	£ million.
Net income from agriculture in 1962	529
,, ,, in secondary and tertiary occupations	672
	1,201

Besides these sources of earned income there are substantial revenues from income from investments, etc., abroad; which have not been included in the above estimates. These revenues constitute, in part at least, a very important additional reserve of savings for investment purposes. If derived from the total available income, the savings needed may therefore constitute less than 6½ per cent.

The table on the next page demonstrates the manner in which the capital outlay and the anticipated savings could be balanced.

6. International Co-operation in Finance

The creation of international corporations in the field of finance, but for other purposes too, to be built up according to the needs of the various regions concerned, appears to be one of the most important measures of co-operation towards the

Capital Needed for Planned Development.	£ million.	£ million annually.	Sources of Finance.	£ million annually.
(1) In Agriculture	1,361		(1) Annual allocations by International financial corporations or governments	45
(2) In Industry, transport and related branches	1,115		(2) 6½ per cent. Savings of net product in Agriculture and net income from industry and tertiary occupations . .	78
	2,476			
Annual Average on the assumption of a twenty years' period of planned development		123		
		123		123

common goal. Certain difficulties will, it is true, arise as to the delimitation of local and international competences in the administration of such bodies, but this is only one of the issues which will then have to be solved. Precedents of the establishment of inter-state bodies for the regulation, supply or pooling of production and markets have been known in the past, too; in future their experience might be useful, provided that dominating group-interests in the formation of such bodies or corporations are eliminated. A remarkable statement on this problem is included in an article in the London bi-monthly *Planning*, describing the new tasks of British foreign policy. It stresses the necessity for removing the traditional motives of international financial bodies and is, in fact, not very different from the thought contained in the proposal by Mr. Feis quoted above. This is what *Planning* says:[1]

> The principles upon which this machinery would work must differ radically from those on which international financial bodies have operated in the past, in two ways: First, the loans should be neither private nor simply inter-governmental but operated through an international clearing system, whose object would be equitable pooling of the burden of international investment; secondly, the criterion should be not whether a given investment is likely to prove financially profitable, but whether it provides the most economical means for relating available resources to the most urgent human needs. This is not to say that its objects would be philanthropic, or that it would impose a burden on the advanced countries for which they would see no return. The return would be none the less important because it would appear in the form,

[1] A broadsheet issued by PEP (Political and Economic Planning), London; vide *Planning*, No. 201, of February 9, 1943, p. 14.

> not of short-term profits appearing on the balance-sheets of the more successful private undertakings, but of a social dividend accruing to the community as a whole—new and expanding markets for producers, greater security of employment for workers, and a heightened sense of political and social security for all.

The work of the international corporations in the field of finance would have to be linked to the planning of investment, the latter in turn being based on the new policy of consumption and of raising the income. Increase in consumption, which is the aim of that policy, should manifest itself in the various fields of consumption goods : foodstuffs, means for the production of food, building material, clothing, articles used in the sphere of health and education, etc. The preceding chapters contain calculations relative to the required increase in the production of the principal consumption goods as well as in the purchasing power of the consumer. It is not claimed that these data should be regarded as final or as sufficiently refined to be able to serve as factual material for immediate use. The purpose was to show the necessity for as well as the feasibility of a planned approach in the order of magnitude indicated. To carry out schemes of this kind and size, recourse must be had to the methods and experience of other countries as well as to local experience and researches. Existent machinery will have to be employed alongside with new institutions yet to be created. Their work should be on the lines already tried and tested during the war in the performance of important tasks in the field of supply. As far as the Middle East area is concerned, the name of the Middle East Supply Centre has repeatedly been mentioned as one of the regional centres to be entrusted with the functions of post-war development. There can be no doubt that the Middle East Supply Centre, which has rendered valuable services during the war, can contribute in an important manner towards the solution of the reconstruction problems of the Middle East. But it appears that the all-round development of such destitute regions as are found in the Orient calls for a more comprehensive apparatus than has hitherto been in existence. Besides the need for co-ordinating the work of the international and regional machinery, there is the problem of finding men capable of conceiving and carrying out the necessary operations. This problem could be solved through training and the selection of the best brains available in the regions concerned. The measure of co-operation achieved between them and the local governments as well as the international agencies will be the decisive factor for the success or otherwise of the envisaged schemes.

As for the development activities themselves, which consist of both research and practical work, the establishment of regional bodies would be required. These should divide their tasks in the following manner:

(1) *Agriculture:*
- Irrigation;
- Intensification;
- Draining and reclamation of land;
- Problems of land tenure;
- Improvement of farming (seeds, stock-breeding, manure, etc.);
- Agricultural credits;
- Agricultural research and experimentation.

(2) *Transport:*
- Road building;
- Intra-urban traffic;
- Roads traffic;
- Railways;
- Shipping;
- Air-borne traffic.

(3) *Building and Housing:*
- Rural building;
- Urban building;
- Industrial building.

(4) *Industry:*
- Production of consumption goods;
- Production of capital goods;
- Exploitation of natural resources;
- Electrification;
- Training of technical experts and skilled workers.

(5) *Problems of Distribution:*
- Organization of local trade;
- Organization of foreign trade;
- Nutrition policy and schemes;
- Regional trade agreements;
- Tariff policy.

(6) *Problems concerned with the Finance of Planned Development.*

It must be admitted from the outset that without a certain measure of belief in the feasibility of such far-reaching schemes, they could probably not be tackled. But this belief is not based on theoretical speculations alone. The Western world has a vital interest in helping the less-developed countries to catch up, and to do so in accordance with a well-conceived plan. Fears of a recurrence of the cut-throat competition witnessed on Oriental markets during the past decade seem to be baseless in view of the tremendous increase in the capacity for consumption, which constitutes the principal objective of the new development policy.

The foreign capital that was sunk in Oriental lands in the past has yielded a good return to its investors. Future investments, though perhaps less profitable as far as cash returns are concerned, will, no doubt, turn out to be infinitely more lucrative in other respects.

CHAPTER VIII

THE POSITION OF PALESTINE

No development plan for the economic reconstruction of the Middle East can be drawn up without special attention being devoted to the economic problems arising out of the peculiar position of Palestine as the country of the Jewish National Home. A separate chapter on this point appears justified in view of the unique conditions prevailing in Palestine and their potential importance for other Oriental countries.

What features provide Palestine with her peculiar economic aspects, and invest the latter with an importance reaching far beyond her limited area?

Palestine is, to begin with, the only Oriental country the population of which is made up to a considerable extent of recent immigrants from Europe, who have transformed the economic and social structure of their ancient home. This process has virtually westernized large parts of the country; in the economic sphere its manifestations are the development of natural resources, the raising of productivity in agriculture and industry, and the all-round introduction of progressive methods of work and means of production and distribution. No other country of the Middle East, as we shall soon see, is able to point to an advance so remarkable as that of Palestine; thereby proving the applicability of Western science and thought to an Oriental country.

But there is a second aspect and despite its political implications, which do not need to be gone into here, we cannot afford to neglect it. Palestine has emerged as the only place where Jewish mass settlement was and is a striking success in modern times. In spite of obstacles and discouragement, Jewish efforts in agriculture, industry, transport, etc., have grown in scope and importance; and although numerically inferior, the Jewish sector has become the motive power in the economic life of the country. The achievements attained justify the expectation that given preliminary economic and financial planning, a far larger immigration can be absorbed in Palestine. The possibility of contributing to the solution of a very urgent problem lends particular weight to the demand for the fullest possible utilization of the country's absorptive power; more especially as other nations have so far not been able to offer any genuine solution. From the economic point of view the absorption of a vast Jewish immigration in Palestine is no longer a dream. Given the means and the possibility of directing the economic policy of the country in accordance with modern concepts, such a task should not offer insoluble problems. The size of immigration becomes largely a function of the available capital.

Yet even from the viewpoint of the peoples of the Orient themselves, the presence in their midst of a European population should be valued as a by no means trifling asset. Numerically the addition of one to two million Jews to the population of the Middle East, though completely changing the ratio of peoples in Palestine, would not greatly change the total Oriental population of 1962, which should comprise no less than about 40 million Arabs. True, the pre-war years in Palestine did not witness much co-operation within the country, but the problem might be approached from a different angle. No better witness can be adduced than the champion of freedom for the Arab nations, who expressed himself in visionary words on the potentialities of economic development in Oriental countries through Jewish immigration. Twenty-two years ago, T. E. Lawrence wrote the following words on the task of the Jews in Palestine and in the Oriental world :

> . . . They hope to adjust their mode of life to the climate of Palestine, and by the exercise of their skill and capital to make it as highly organized as a European state. The success of their scheme will involve inevitably the raising of the present Arab population to their own material level, only a little after themselves in point of time, and the consequences might be of the highest importance for the future of the Arab world.

An article which appeared in the Mecca paper *Al Qibla*, No. 183, of March 23, 1918, and which was attributed by the late George Antonius to King Hussein himself, contained the following passages :

> The resources of the country are still virgin soil, and will be developed by the labour and capital of the Jewish immigrants. . . . One of the most amazing things till recent times was that the Palestinian used to leave this country, wandering over the high seas in every direction. His native soil could not retain him, though his ancestors had lived on it for over a thousand years. And, at the same time, we saw the Jews from foreign countries streaming to Palestine from Russia, Germany, Austria, Spain, America . . . The cause of causes could not escape those who had

> the gift of a deeper insight; they knew that that country was for its original sons (*abna'ihi-l-asliyin*), for all their differences, a sacred and beloved homeland. Experience has proved their capacity to succeed in their energies and their labours. . . . The return of these exiles (*jaliya*) to their homeland will prove materially and spiritually an experimental school for their brethren (i.e. the Arabs) who are with them in the fields, factories, trades, and in all things connected with toil and labour.

These words were a remarkable forecast of the potential effects of Jewish immigration in the economic sphere. In the light of the experience of the period between the two wars, this belief of men with an understanding of the East has shown itself to be fully justified.

The following is a very summary description of the main economic features introduced by Jews in Palestine, which might prove of importance for other Oriental countries as well.

1. The Agrarian Sector

Palestine's agriculture was formerly conducted on the basis of extensive, primitive, and scarcely profitable grain-growing, primarily for the requirements of the Fellahin. Only in certain climatically favoured districts and in the vicinity of the towns was a higher level achieved. This culture is now paralleled and in part replaced by a highly intensive, technically and economically rationalized agricultural sector. In the course of experiments lasting for many years, and after numerous setbacks, a system of mixed farming has been developed which enables the farmers to maintain from their own farms a far higher standard of life than that of the Fellah, albeit this has involved large investments. The new forms of enterprise which have been evolved are novel in both their social and economic structure. They are based on the application or combination of the following factors:

(i) The introduction and increasing employment of new biological and technical means and devices. One of the outstanding features is the development of a new crop rotation system replacing the centuries-old primitive succession of crops in the local agriculture. It affords a higher degree of exploitation of the soil without robbing it of its nutritive qualities, and enables the farmer to achieve a better balance between the needs of men, animals and land on his farm. In modernized grain production, machines have largely replaced manual labour. Tractors and combines, i.e. combined cutting and threshing machines, largely replace draught animals and human labour in grain farming, and permit the surmounting of the recurrent difficulties of harvest due to climatic conditions, shortage of labour, etc. In fodder and vegetable cultivation irrigation is now conducted on an ever-increasing scale by automatic water-sprayers, which demand nothing more than a few turns of the wrist. Modern incubators, rationally built sheds for cattle with all associated provisions for feeding and cleaning, not only save human labour but extend the life of the equipment and livestock.

(ii) The livestock itself has been considerably improved by the introduction of high-yield milch-cows, high-yield sheep and pure-bred chickens. The level of productivity in milk and egg production lies far above that of native production, and has permitted this branch to become a vital constituent of modern agriculture in Palestine. The same applies, *mutatis mutandis*, to the use of selected seed varieties, which increase both yield and resistance to pests, etc. etc.

(iii) The discovery and rational exploitation of large underground water resources has become of particular importance for the evaluation of the country's absorptive capacity. The utilization of sub-surface water along modern lines in regions which were never before held suitable for irrigated crops has very considerably influenced the plans of settlement and development in such areas. It has also reduced the cost per water unit used and has simplified the problem of profitability. In regions with inadequate rainfall the tapping of underground water has been the main factor permitting settlement, thus transforming steppe lands into flourishing cultivated areas.

(iv) The most important result of this progress as far as concerns settlement policy is that the area required for the settlement of a family has been reduced, thus permitting an increase in the density of settlement, i.e. in the number of settlers on a given area. An area of 100 dunams (= 25 acres) in the Palestine Coastal Plain, which formerly afforded a meagre existence to a Fellah family of five, can provide four to five families with a living, given adequate water supply for irrigation. This has converted Palestine, a relatively limited area, into a territory whose capacity for absorbing settlers is as yet far from exhausted.

(v) The complicated problems of marketing and price in a country with differing standards of living and wages have been largely solved by means of co-operative organization. Perishable products of Jewish agriculture pass from producer to consumer through a well-developed network of delivery stations and sales stores. Modern installations of refrigerators for potatoes, etc., help to alleviate the problem of storage in a warm climate.

(vi) Finally, the continued extension of agricultural, educational and research facilities through the establishment of agricultural institutes and schools also calls for mention. Institutions devoted to agricultural research as well as a network of schools from the secondary school to the university, provide the theoretical knowledge necessary for the conduct of agriculture and the study of its problems.

2. The Industrial Sector

Prior to the outbreak of the Second World War the industrial development of Palestine could not show any striking figures of production or employment comparable with those of other countries undergoing the industrialization process, and certainly not with those of established industrial countries. The total value of annual production in handicrafts and industry barely exceeded £10 million, while the number of workers scarcely equalled that to be found in a middle-sized industrial town in Europe or America.

Nevertheless the industrial economy of this country manifests a number of specific characteristics which differentiate it from those of the surrounding Oriental countries. Whereas industry has been very strongly promoted by the Government in Turkey and Iran, and to some degree in Egypt as well (in the two former countries the largest industrial undertakings are either state enterprises or belong to the state banks), all industrial experiments in Palestine were undertaken by private initiative and enterprise, only gradually receiving some moderate protection from the Government. It must remain questionable whether all of the new national industries of the former countries, which have developed in, so to speak, a hot-house atmosphere, could have maintained themselves under such conditions of free competition as those to which the youthful Palestinian industry has largely had to adapt itself. This, however, is not the only point with regard to which Palestine's industrial economy differs from those of the other Oriental territories. The Jewish industrial sector, which comprehends the majority of the industrial undertakings and employees of the country, is based entirely on the employment of labour recompensed according to European standards.

The consequences are remarkable. Palestine alone has a body of workers organized on a Trade Union basis and including the majority of the workers, under whose pressure modern relations between employer and employed are established on a basis of free contract. Hence conditions here are being adapted more rapidly than in neighbouring lands to those of industrial countries in which the worker is regarded not as an object of undisturbed exploitation but as an important partner in the productive process.

The many experts who had lost the basis of their existence in Europe before the war on account of political developments, and who became available for work in Palestine, have benefited the youthful industry of the country and enabled it to develop in an unforeseen fashion. In certain cases the exceptional inventiveness and adaptability of these specialists have led to technical achievements and successes which permanently enrich the country's economic power.

The results of this state of affairs have been plain to see during the present war. No Oriental country was in a position to adjust its industry to the special requirements of the War Effort to the same degree as Palestine. The scale of orders from the military authorities has grown rapidly. For 1942 it has already been estimated at £8 million with a total production value for the year of £30–35 million, despite the fact that numerous branches of industry have been affected by the shortage of raw materials, machinery, etc.

If we endeavour to isolate the particular features upon which Palestine's industry is based, and as a result of which it is in a position to provide a lesson for the neighbouring countries, we find the following :

(i) The degree of productivity in the new industry is very considerable and, in a number of branches, exceeds that of the corresponding enterprises in neighbouring countries per worker employed. This superiority is due to the greater experience of the owners and directors of the undertakings, who were frequently able to transfer their factories entire from Europe to Palestine ; and in addition to the greater dexterity and efficiency of the workers themselves.

(ii) A special feature is the adaptation of Jewish industry to the need for implements and apparatus for purposes of production. It is a normal trend that industrial production in a mature country turns increasingly to capital goods, i.e. goods for production and not for consumption. These tendencies are already observable in Palestine, and the list of such goods, a few years ago rather a modest one, now grows quickly, more especially under the impact of the war, and shows a remarkable variety of production tools. There is every reason to believe in the possibilities of maintaining part at least of this production in peace-time.

(iii) The far-reaching independence of state support and promotion characterizing this youthful industry, in fact the necessity of surmounting obstacles met with in the course of development, has trained the persons engaged in the industrialization of Palestine to find their own feet. As a result, initiative has developed far more than in the other countries, where the state itself stands behind industrialization or carries it through from above.

(iv) Finally, the comprehensive organization of the workers and the relations between employers and labour have regulated the procedure in labour conflicts and have facilitated their adjustment. At the same time the relatively high standard of living of the worker in Palestine, deriving as it does from the existence of Labour organization, is a prerequisite for the purchasing power of the population, which has been able to absorb a large part of its own production.

CHAPTER IX

THE PROBLEM OF AN ORIENTAL FEDERATION

Plans for the economic reconstruction of the Middle East cannot ignore the world-wide tendency towards unification of small states within the larger unit of a union. There is no doubt that the establishment of a Federation of Oriental Nations, which has not infrequently been discussed in recent years, is in line with the general trend of ideas about an improved political order in the world. But we have to examine the consequences of such a union for our Oriental countries, before applying a formula that has proved suitable for other regions.

What would be the economic effect of a union of states in the Middle East? Among the problems arising in this connection, those related to the establishment of a uniform customs territory hold pride of place. One of the first criteria of political suzerainty over a territory is the uniform administration of its customs policy, and the establishment of a single customs system over the entire area of the country. A uniform customs policy enables the Central Authorities to influence the economic development of a country in a most effective way and in accordance with definite principles.

In a federation the body which determines the customs policy, administrative procedure and tariff system must have the power of issuing prescriptions binding upon the authorities of the associated countries, and of punishing any disregard of instructions. At the same time it is inevitable that the implications of the issues handled by the body responsible for tariff policy must extend far beyond fiscal problems in the more restricted sense. Customs policy influences state finances, the development of trade and industry, money and currency, traffic —in brief all those spheres which are of importance for the economic well-being of the State as a whole.

With the exception of Palestine most of the countries of the Middle East manifest an economic life which has virtually uniform characteristics, despite all differences in geography and climate. The fact of a dry climate, that is, of a long summer without rain, and the need for artificial irrigation in the regions without rainfall, has produced parallel vegetal and productive conditions over extensive zones of the Orient. In addition, a number of social, political and juridical factors have led to largely uniform foundations for economic development. These include the institutions of Moslem Law, the development of a feudal system with certain forms that are specific for Western Asia, and the Ottoman régime which imposed its politics and administration upon these areas.

If the area to be united under a single Customs Policy is limited to the three or four countries Palestine, Syria and Lebanon, Transjordan, and possibly Iraq, it will soon be found that a task which is in itself none too difficult will be greatly complicated. The economic development of one of these countries, namely Palestine, has since the last war followed a course entirely different from that of the others. As against the relatively self-contained development to be observed in the economic life of countries like Syria and Iraq, Palestine outgrew its previous economic life, which had once been proportionate to that of the neighbouring countries. Economic conditions, the activities in trade and industry, the degree of development in agriculture and traffic, the employment of improved methods of production and distribution, all of these criteria of the stage of development of a national economy showed that other forms of organization and stages of economic progress had been created in Palestine, and particularly within its Jewish sector. Hence the inclusion of Palestine in a Customs Union with the neighbouring Arab countries would, in the case of the establishment of a uniform Customs Policy, either very considerably affect the equilibrium as well as the growth of the Jewish economy, in case the uniform customs system is oriented towards the requirements of the Arab countries or, on the contrary, would not pay sufficient attention to the requirements of the said Arab countries if the demands of the progressive Jewish economic development were to be given primary consideration. In a sense, similar doubts may be entertained, for the time being at least, in regard to the relation between the Lebanon and the less urbanized Arab countries.

Transjordan, to take an extreme case, is interested in the cheap provision of industrial products while, at the same time, wishing the conditions of production for cereals, and in particular for wheat, to be as favourable as possible. As against this, industrial Palestine, which is largely identical with Jewish industry, is interested in the cheap supply of cereals and the restriction, in principle, of cheap imports of industrial articles that can be produced within the country. The same applies to the industrial sector of the Lebanon.

Before this war Palestine imported vast quantities of foodstuffs and raw materials, whereas Iraq, Syria and Egypt were large-scale exporters of foodstuffs and raw materials. This difference in the foreign trade is the outcome of the different economic structures and trends in the countries concerned. There is not as yet any marked shift in the occupational distribution of the population of Arab countries at the expense of agriculture. Palestine, however, offers another picture. The number of secondary producers in this country exceeds by far the proportion to be found in other Oriental lands. Palestine was able to build up a very remarkable capacity for industrial production. Such a capacity is not an asset that should be frittered away ; it should, on the contrary, be well nursed in order to be able to serve such a tremendous realm as the agrarian zone of the Middle East. The promising industrial enterprises of Palestine and other Oriental countries have a claim—as each industry has in the initial stages of its development—to encouraging treatment. Palestine has hitherto been dependent for its industrial sector on the supply of cereals and other foodstuffs as well as raw materials and machinery, and it will remain so for a long time to come. Oriental countries have derived much profit from this situation for the last decade ; they have supplied materials to a value of £21·4 million while importing from Palestine no more than for £4·5 million. (See also table on next page.) These figures will increase considerably in the future, when the development outlined has assumed a more definite shape. Industrialization, it is true, constitutes an important aim of most Oriental countries, and in view of the anticipated increase in the power of consumption nobody needs to worry about the future of industrial production in Oriental countries. But as regards Palestine and areas showing similar features a more cautious approach is required. In their case, owing to the high wage level of local labour, a large part of the industrial production would be threatened by competition as a result of the cheaply produced articles brought from abroad.

The central problem in trade between Oriental countries consists of the following : In view of the extremely low share of human labour in production costs in less developed regions, branches of production requiring a high proportion of unskilled labour must of necessity be accorded some measure of protection in countries with a higher wage level.

From this it follows that the establishment of a Customs Union as an outcome of Federal Union involves serious consideration of the fate of important economic branches in the member states of the Federation, and particularly in Palestine.

IMPORT AND EXPORT BETWEEN PALESTINE AND THE NEIGHBOURING COUNTRIES (EGYPT, SYRIA-LEBANON, TURKEY AND IRAQ) 1931–40 [1]

Import into / Export from } Palestine.	Food, Drink and Tobacco.	Raw Materials.	Manufactured Articles.	Total.*
1931 Import from the four countries	987,050	128,474	737,306	1,852,830
Export to ,, ,, ,,	157,537	40,750	200,537	398,824
1932 Import from the four countries	1,067,908	138,194	630,695	1,836,797
Export to ,, ,, ,,	144,719	22,240	193,286	360,245
1933 Import from the four countries	1,372,476	128,435	533,474	2,034,385
Export to ,, ,, ,,	101,037	17,117	170,045	288,199
1934 Import from the four countries	1,353,074	159,749	528,345	2,041,168
Export to ,, ,, ,,	112,039	32,315	152,792	297,146
1935 Import from the four countries	1,451,859	212,993	666,931	2,331,783
Export to ,, ,, ,,	137,765	57,329	197,137	392,231
1936 Import from the four countries	1,662,100	118,578	484,064	2,264,742
Export to ,, ,, ,,	157,006	105,888	168,268	431,162
1937 Import from the four countries	1,675,050	155,444	759,439	2,589,933
Export to ,, ,, ,,	394,244	221,152	234,188	849,584
1938 Import from the four countries	1,055,082	100,995	493,407	1,649,484
Export to ,, ,, ,,	232,220	138,852	195,109	566,181
1939 Import from the four countries	1,445,853	182,973	613,877	2,242,703
Export to ,, ,, ,,	235,487	89,843	174,950	500,280
1940 Import from the four countries	1,769,617	423,353	387,358	2,580,328
Export to ,, ,, ,,	199,049	59,038	181,605	439,692
Total Import from the four countries	13,840,069	1,749,188	5,834,896	21,424,153
Total Export to the four countries	1,871,103	784,524	1,867,917	4,523,544

* Totals refer to classified goods only, the grand totals for the decade in question being LP.23,092,617 and LP.4,539,003 for imports and exports respectively.

From the viewpoint of economic resources and size of population, the large countries of the Middle East, functioning as they do at a low level, outweigh other more developed zones within it. There can be scarcely any doubt that the achievements of those areas which have attained a high standard of productivity and living would be seriously threatened by indiscriminate treatment or pooling of economic resources and positions within the framework of one federation. An adjustment of the divergent levels could be enforced only at the expense of the more developed parts of Oriental populations.

[1] During this period there were some changes in the mode of registration, which, however, do not essentially affect the final results. As regards Transjordan, Palestine trade statistics give no complete picture.

Comparative Data on Oriental Economies

	Egypt.	Syria.	Iraq.	Turkey.	Palestine.		
					Arabs.	Jews.	Total Population.
National income in £ per head (1936)	12	13	10	19	16	46	26
Wages in Industry (1933–35) in mils per head per day	60–150	100–150	40–75	80–100	100–350	200–500	
Agriculture: Productivity per male worker 1934–5 in I.U.	90	97	93	104	186	683	251
Wages (1933–5) in mils per head per day . .	20–50	40–100	20–40	40–50	80–200	200–400	
Wheat in 100 kg. per ha. (1937) .	21·5	8·4	7·3	10·8	6	12	
State Finance (1938–9): Revenue in £ p.h.	2·323	0·894	2·119	3·286			3·958
Expenditure in £ p.h.	2·494	0·788	2·198	2·958			3·870
Capital Investment p.h. of working population in £— in Agriculture .	19	—	—	—	—	69	
in Building . .	31	—	—	—	—	201	
in Railways . .	4·9	6·8	10·3	7·5	—	—	10·4
Import per head: Average of 1936–8 in £ . . .	2·19	1·84	2·38	1·14	4·07	24·85	10·50
Export per head: Average of 1936–8 in £ . . .	2·10	0·91	1·16	1·28	2·60	8·73	3·44
Natural Increase (1931–5) per 1,000	14·9	—	—	—	24·97	20·91	23·71
Infant Mortality (1931–5) per 1,000	165–208*	—	312†	—	166	78	151
Density of Traffic: Number of motor vehicles per 1,000 persons (1938) .	2·1	3·0	1·9	0·6	—	—	6·2
Railway Lines: Length in km. per 10,000 persons (1938) . . .	3·1	3·9	3·3	4·2	—	—	5·3

* The first figure (165) refers to the whole country; the second (208) refers only to localities having a Health Bureau, where registration is more complete.

† This figure refers to Baghdad, Mosul and Basra only.

…ly …age …ree …rs).	Import: Foodstuffs and Live Animals.	Import: Materials, Raw or Partly Manu-factured.	Import: Manu-factured Articles.	Import: Total.	Per Head of Total Population.	Export: Foodstuffs and Live Animals.	Export: Materials, Raw or Partly Manu-factured.	Export: Manu-factured Articles.	Export: Total.
5–8	5,522 5	15,045 13	98,299 82	118,866 100	LT. 7·07	50,941 38	79,533 60	3,080 2	133,5… 100
6–8	447 23	180 9	1,341 68	1,968 100	£ 5·27	693 35	1,251 62	59 3	2,0… 100
6–8	3,921 27	1,239 8	9,548 65	14,708† 100	LP. 10·50	4,034 84	247 5	538 11	4,8… 100
5–7	3,990 12	10,180 30	19,670 58	33,876‡ 100.	£E. 2·14	4,000 11	30,393 86	860 3	35,2… 100
6–8	1,120 13	7,581 87		8,701 100	I.D. 2·38	2,659 63	1,588 37		4,2… 100
6–8	8,381 17	39,809 83		48,190 100	£LS. 13·50	12,014 51	11,754 49		23,7… 100
6–8	417,823 45	270,336 29	240,540 26	932,399‖ 100	£19 10s. 7d.	37,612 8	57,632 12	370,314 78	477,6… 100
6–8	1,885,067 37	2,729,467 54	430,566 9	5,045,100 100	GM 68·30	78,966 2	968,700 18	4,264,200 80	5,311,8… 100
6–8	10,343,464 27	21,912,368 38	5,667,532 15	37,923,364 100	Ffrs. 904	3,413,078 15	7,569,659 32	12,343,266 53	23,326,0… 100
6–8	190,110 12	311,791 21	977,402 65	1,504,519¶ 100	Rs. 4·09	402,198 22	857,632 48	509,034 28	1,799,9… 100

…various currency units see table on page x. † Including NAAFI and Military Stores in the amount of L…
…ssified goods amounting to £E. 36,000 in respect of Imports and £E. 67,000 in respect of Exports.
…and excluding crude petroleum exported by the Iraq Petroleum Co.
…l post to the value of £3,700,000 Import and £12,106,000 Export.
…assified goods and parcel post : Rs. 25,216,000 Import and Rs. 31,050,000 Export.

Hence the establishment of a federation between the states involved would obviously not achieve one of the most important aims proclaimed in the new programmes of economic reconstruction, namely the promotion of welfare and the raising of the living standard.

This does not mean that the sound element in the concept of a federation has no chance of realization in the Middle East. Customs unions have, as a rule, grown or been formed after economic conditions in the potential member states have become more and more uniform. This is a slow process of economic, social and political development. If, for cogent reasons, the early establishment of a federation should be advisable, it should be effected in such a way as to reduce to a minimum the possibilities of harm which might result from a sudden forcing of the countries in question into a fiscal and economic union. In other words, the necessary time must be given for the development of a more homogeneous economic structure. If then, in accordance with our general planning concepts, higher levels have been attained in *all* member states, the right time may be considered to have come for the establishment of a genuine federation.

CHAPTER X

CONCLUSION

After describing the interrelation of the various factors and their relative importance in the dynamics of economic progress in the Orient, we were able to suggest the broad outlines for the planned development of Oriental economy. We were, of course, aware of the limitations and obstacles which any planning policy will have to face in the countries of the Middle East. We have already referred to some of them in the foregoing chapters. Reconstruction in Oriental countries means a carefully conceived and gradually increasing direction of economic activity. To achieve this an elastic system of governmental guidance and control is required, linked to international agencies working along the same lines ; something not too rigid in its conception, and adapted to the local conditions in each case. Individual methods for each country or region will have to be adopted and varied according to the situation ; while different periods will be needed for efficiently carrying out the projects selected for execution.

What has been defined by us as the principal aim in such a systematic and active guidance of a people's economic life? It is the establishment of a higher standard of living for the common man as regards nutrition, housing, clothing, education and health. We have reached the conclusion that these aims can be realized while maintaining a well-considered economic policy which utilizes all the expedients of the modern state in the field of finance, the organization of governmental services and publicly-owned enterprises and the like. Fortunately, general economic tendencies in Oriental countries as well as in the Western hemisphere seem to be moving in this direction ; but we can scarcely afford to wait until these tendencies achieve complete realization. Nor, to our belief, would they achieve it, if unguided, in a manner compatible with the generally accepted standards of the West. It is necessary to accelerate them and to direct their course in order that the Oriental world may be adjusted more rapidly to those material conditions of life which are regarded, if not as ideal standards, at least as adequate by Western civilization.

It is our considered opinion that the governments of the

Oriental countries, if they so desire, have the power to effect the necessary changes.

Our point of departure was that any improvement in the standard of living must commence with the peasant, who is the basic element of the Oriental population. The measures proposed by us are : (i) Redistribution of national income through reduction of rent on land, reform of land tenure, policy of taxation for the benefit of the lower income groups, and the introduction of improved marketing methods ; (ii) Raising productivity and extension of cultivated area through the inauguration of large-scale development projects, with special reference to irrigated farming ; (iii) Industrialization as a definite state policy ; (iv) Restricting the tendencies towards world-market price fluctuations and their effects on local production by means of international agreements ; (v) Establishment of state services on a large scale in the sphere of communications, health, education, etc.

We have been able to demonstrate the financial order of magnitude involved when a comprehensive scheme of modern housing and nutrition is envisaged. The amounts needed appear formidable at first glance, but the state of poverty in existence is no less so, and it would be a travesty of all promises to establish a better order of things if the majority of the population in these old countries, the cradle of our civilization, were to be left in their misery and distress.

But, what seems to us even more important in this connection, we have also been able to demonstrate that by a policy of planned development the resources of these countries can be easily expanded, so as to increase the productivity and the real income of the lower classes. The expenditure involved in raising the standard of living, as well as the cost of better housing, could be met from the increase in agrarian productivity as well as through the execution of public works and development schemes. The financing of the no less vital educational and health programmes, which may be carried out in accordance with the experience of more developed Western states, does not appear to present a complicated problem for a progressive policy of taxation. The amounts involved are trifling when compared with those needed for raising the standard of living. The main issue of finance, the procuring of the huge sums needed for capital investments, has to be handled along the accepted lines of international co-operation in the development of backward areas.

The establishment of a minimum standard of nutrition and its adaptation to the specific climatic conditions and habits of the various countries does not in itself constitute a solution of the problem of under-nourishment, nor does a demonstration of the existence of potential areas of production solve the problem of distribution. This holds good particularly as regards the economical execution of schemes for improved nutrition, though the increase in purchasing power in Middle Eastern countries and the vast stretches of unused land described above will greatly facilitate such a task. The question of a uniform approach to the issues of international agrarian policy is still in its first stages. The solution calls for world-wide organisational measures covering international and local marketing conditions. In the past such measures were usually taken by the producers' cartels, which were in a position to impose their interests on those of the consumers and gain the help of their governments for this purpose. This method, which will scarcely prove feasible after the war, either in the Orient or in Western countries, will have to be replaced by some other, more adequate to the needs of the community at large.

Such a change can be brought about through a policy shaped by a balanced consideration of the interests of producers and consumers alike. In this connection the experience gained in the present war with regard to the organization of nutrition should prove of great importance. Claims for such a world-wide reorganization of consumption and production are gaining ground. The most far-reaching economic outcome of the exigencies of war is that the State has become a regulating and planning authority, and has been able to collect valuable experience in this field. Such organizational experience must be utilized, apart from the plans for production schemes, in order to offer guidance to a policy of consumption aiming at the establishment of a minimum standard in nutrition, housing and clothing. This is a demand which has been accepted as a general postulate in numerous official utterances; and by no means unimportant organizational beginnings before as well as during this war offer prospects of successful continuation and extension.

One fact emerges from the observation of the most recent phase of economic and social history: experience in Europe and America repeats itself in the East. Any large-scale economic development in the countries of the Middle East is bound automatically to lead to a rise in the standard of living, and the maintenance of any such rise on a broad scale is again dependent upon such an economic development. But one should not overlook the great difference between the position of the less-advanced Oriental countries and that of the Western world. Reconstruction in the sense of securing better or more equal conditions of life is, in the West, not necessarily connected with increased production in agriculture and industry; it appears that sometimes the reverse might be more correctly contended. The centre of gravity of a new economic order in mature countries must therefore be sought in a regulation of the productive forces, in the harnessing of economic resource and, it goes without saying, in a better distribution of national income.

The key for a regeneration of the countries of the Middle East, on the other hand, definitely lies in an increase of total production and productivity per head and the opening up of new resources. And there is another point. One of the gravest features of modern economic development in the West was periodical unemployment; it offered a terrible contrast to the immense power of production released by several generations of human inventiveness. The East has not yet had to face any serious apparition of this problem. But it has paid a heavy price for its belated appearance within the orbit of the industrial revolution; namely, the economic and social backwardness of most of its inhabitants. The task facing the leading statesmen of Middle East countries as well as the international bodies concerned with reconstruction problems in this area, is to prepare them for the impact of industrialization and rationalized agriculture. Many as were the triumphs achieved in the material world, the Western countries nevertheless failed to solve the problems arising out of the new industrial age. The tremors shaking the body and soul of Europe for decades are a clear sign of this. It is possibly no mere coincidence that the Jews, who are being expelled in so terrible a fashion from Europe as a consequence of the aggravated crisis of the Old World, now find themselves in Western Asia at the prècise moment when this sub-continent enters upon a new phase in its history.

The industrial revolution in Europe was the result of new lines of human thought and inventiveness. Its shortcomings and deficiencies in the later stages were in a sense the outcome of inadequate human foresight or willingness to check the dangers inherent in the machine. The transformation of the Orient and the securing of better social and economic conditions, calls first and foremost for the presence and co-operation of a human element, in fairly large numbers, who are willing and competent to act as pioneers of this process ; also for a definite policy on the part of the State aiming at the identical goal. It now happens that .the tremendous possibilities which exist in the Middle East for absorbing huge numbers of newcomers offer precisely those conditions prerequisite for the solution of one of of the most urgent problems of contemporary mankind. Obviously the world has not yet realized the full extent of these immense possibilities. But it should now recognize that these neglected spaces can be brought to new life by utilizing the creative capacities of those who were once a, if not the, spiritual driving force of the Orient.

APPENDIX I

THE AGRICULTURAL ABSORPTIVE CAPACITY OF MIDDLE EASTERN COUNTRIES

The term " living space ", which has been so widely used in the political discussions of Europe since the last war, derives primarily from the political and economic situation within Europe itself. Political progaganda made the expression its own and, by skilful exploitation of the unsatisfactory relations in Central Europe after the war, helped considerably to exacerbate the international situation.

The slogan of insufficient living space has also penetrated into the Orient. If, however, the premises on which the term is based are highly questionable in Europe, they are even more so in the East. Here human life is overshadowed by the sense of vast open spaces, and densely populated areas are, with the exception of Egypt, largely conspicuous by their absence.

Naturally the density of population varies considerably from one part of the Orient to another. To begin with, Egypt, which a century ago had a very small population, has seen this population undergo a five- or six-fold increase over the figures of the commencement of the nineteenth century ; their subsistence, meagre as it is, was made possible thanks to the care devoted to irrigation development during the century. In other Oriental areas, however, such as Syria, Iraq, Transjordan, Turkey and Iran, the considerable potentialities offered by the uncultivated or sporadically worked areas have not hitherto been utilized in any measure worthy of mention, although attention has frequently been drawn to these potentialities during recent generations.

The sparse population of this enormous region is even to-day the most striking impression gathered by the observant traveller. Apart from a few areas near the coast or along the main rivers, huge desolate or thinly cultivated stretches, sometimes several thousands of square kilometres in extent, may often be traversed without passing more than a few impoverished villages or nomad encampments. At the same time traces of former habitations dating from ancient days to the not-too-distant past are found on all sides, proclaiming the empty wastes of to-day as the densely populated homes of antique culture and civilization.

This contrast is particularly vivid in some of the territories in Palestine's vicinity. Deep in the steppe regions of Hauran and east of the line Damascus–Aleppo we find innumerable ruins and sites of human habitation beyond the present limits of cultivation, in a region which is to-day generally considered as waste land or desert. Archæological and documentary evidence go to prove that these districts were still populated in the late Hellenic and early Byzantine periods. Similarly in North Syria, where, in the territory lying between Aleppo, Antioch and the Orontes, the remains of what were once flourishing centres of ancient settlement may be found amid to-day's decay. Again, South Palestine, towards the Egyptian frontier (the Negeb), is to-day a wilderness; yet the remains of half a dozen cities have been discovered there, grouped within a comparatively small area. With regard to Mesopotamia where climatic conditions were not as favourable to the preservation of ruins as in the countries of the Mediterranean seaboard, we possess a wealth of documentary evidence testifying to the high level of agriculture and settlement attained in antiquity and continuing into the early Middle Ages. Both the northern part of the state of Iraq and the more southerly Babylonia, where to-day the bulk of the urban and rural population, with the semi-nomad tribes, eke out a meagre existence, were the homes of mighty and densely-populated empires. These regions were in antiquity the scenes of the highest flowering of human civilization. There is no need to delve far back into the past in the case of Anatolia, where traces of yesterday's denser settlement are evident in places now abandoned. The traveller proceeding west from Ankara, Turkey's new capital, is continuously reminded by countless deserted Greek villages that only a short time ago this region held a peasant population numbering many hundreds of thousands. The area utilized for the repatriation of the Turkish and other Moslem peasants from the Balkans comprised only a fraction of the territory freed by the exchange of populations with Greece after 1923.

Both the past history and the present conditions of Middle East territories thus combine to emphasize their potentialities as centres of new settlement. Obviously settlement formulæ cannot be based merely on calculations of area, density of population and similar statistical data that do not take into account the special social, economic and political conditions and difficulties current in the Middle East since the last war. Nevertheless even a theoretical estimate of the areas which may be available for settlement is of great interest and would prove very useful for the forming of judgments as to the agricultural potentialities of the countries in question.

For that purpose it seems appropriate to deal separately with the conditions prevailing in each of the principal Middle Eastern countries.

1. Iraq's Settlement Potentialities

The two most important factors to be considered when measuring settlement capacity are the nature of the soil, in the widest sense of the term, and the existing density of population. From both these points of view, Iraq—the Land of the Two Rivers—seems to offer the greatest promise. The density of population in Iraq is low even in comparison with the low level common to the neighbouring Oriental countries. Its vast cultivation potentialities are indicated by the irrigation opportunities afforded by the great water arteries which cross a large part of the cultivable area, placing it in a privileged position as compared with other Middle East countries which depend mainly on rainfall for their agricultural development. The two prime requirements of land and water are found in Iraq to a degree which endows the country with, for all practical ends, an inexhaustible absorptive capacity.

As much as four-fifths of Iraq's total area, some 360,000 out of 453,000 sq. kms. was in recent years beyond the scope of cultivation.[1] This area comprises mainly the desert and steppe country in the west, south-west and east, the marshlands on the lower river levels and the uplands in the north. Nevertheless there remains an immediately cultivable area of more than 90,000 sq. kms., nearly three times as big as that in Egypt. The amount of land actually under tillage in Iraq was estimated at 78,000 sq. kms.; but only a fraction of this is under continuous cultivation, mainly on account of the very primitive agricultural practice of transferring cultivation to successive areas as the fertility of each is exhausted. The cultivated area in any given agricultural year amounts to not more than a fraction, estimated at 10–20 per cent. of the entire cultivable area. Even where cultivation is regular, for example in the river districts irrigated by pump installations, modern methods are not widely employed.

Since the extent of the irrigable area is of decisive importance

[1] Figures concerning land areas have been drawn from Sir Ernest Dowson's official *Inquiry into Land Tenure and Related Questions*, published in London, 1932.

in estimating agricultural capacity, it may be of interest to refer briefly to figures for areas in the irrigation zones in various parts of the country. Irrigation in Iraq is practised either by gravitation from canals and rivers, where these are situated on levels higher than the irrigated area, or by lifting and pumping where they lie below the surface level. As can be seen from the following table, the total irrigable area amounts at present to 51,000 sq. kms., situated mainly in the south of the country.

APPROXIMATE CLASSIFICATION OF LAND SURFACE IN IRAQ[1]

Liwa (Province).	Total Area.	Partially Cultivated Region.			Additional Potentially Cultivable Territory.	Total Cultivated and Cultivable Territory.	Mean Density per sq. km. of Cultivated Area. (Estim.)†
		Rainfall Zone.	Irrigation Zone.				
		Plains.	Canal-fed Territory.*	Machine-fed Territory.*			
Mosul . . .	45,800	14,580	—	—	270	15,040	22
Arbil . . .	16,600	7,010	—	—	—	7,160	15
Sulimani . .	9,500	2,420	—	—	—	2,550	37
Kirkuk. . .	20,800	12,020	—	—	3,240	15,260	13
Diyala . . .	16,200	710	2,760	90	260	3,820	67
Baghdad . .	22,100	—	1,710	2,270	890	4,870	98
Dulaim . .	124,500	—	920	630	20	1,570	95
Karbala . .	21,200	—	660	—	20	680	—
Hilla . . .	8,100	—	4,570	330	1,630	6,530	21
Kut . . .	16,400	—	4,680	3,860	2,170	10,710	20
Diwaniya . .	83,000	—	3,770	2,180	5,520	11,470	40
Muntafiq . .	38,700	—	4,440	270	370	5,080	72
Amara . .	19,700	—	5,670	1,010	—	6,680	36
Basra . . .	10,900	—	610‡	60	110	780	284
Total . .	453,500	36,740	29,790	10,700	14,500	92,200	36

* Territories so classified are at present very incompletely irrigated.
† Refers to the region of 78,000 sq. kms. partly cultivated land.
‡ Tidally watered date gardens.

The cultivable area in the northern part of the country, where agriculture depends on rainfall alone, may be estimated at 41,000 sq. kms. The density of population in the cultivable (and in part cultivated) area in 1930 averaged 36 inhabitants per square kilometre.[2] For the rural population the non-irrigated area shows a density figure of 19 inhabitants per square kilometre, while the irrigated areas show 35 per square kilometre; which is far lower than the density figures of other settled areas in the Middle East.

[1] Figures according to Dowson.
[2] Meanwhile the figures for density may have risen by 20–25 per cent.

A comparison of Iraq's density figures with those of other countries (see table p. 145) indicates the great settlement possibilities of its irrigable areas and points to its capacity to support an enormous additional population.

Population Deficiency

Not only is there ample room for additional population in Iraq, but the present number of inhabitants has been recognized as so small as to inhibit the progress of the country. The need for an increased population as a condition for Iraq's advance has been stressed by many Iraqi statesmen. In a paper prepared in 1926 for the Royal Central Asian Society, Ja'far Pasha al Askari, the then Prime Minister, stated :

> The size of the country is 150,000 sq. miles, which is about three times that of England and Wales, whilst the population is only 3 millions. In the Nile Valley, from Aswan to the sea, where you get a riverain population living upon irrigated lands, there are some 13 million inhabitants. The possible irrigable area in Iraq is certainly not less than that of Egypt.
>
> We may start off by saying, therefore, that what Iraq wants above everything else is more population. This is a necessary condition of progress.

A striking illustration of the particular difficulties arising in Iraq from the small size of its population has been provided in recent years. The wider application of oil pumps for irrigation and the establishment of numerous new irrigated farms led only to a shifting of the agricultural population, attracted from other areas of the country where they forsook their former cultivation. The Report on the *Progress of Iraq* during the period 1920–31, submitted by the British Government to the League of Nations at the termination of the Iraq Mandate, contains the following comment on this point :

> So many of the new irrigated farms were initiated that the already gravely insufficient agricultural population was attracted from established agriculture to these new ventures. Such a movement is bound to have serious economic and social consequences owing to the relatively small agricultural population of the country. It is probable that the able-bodied male agricultural population of the country is less than 500,000. Schemes such as new irrigation projects or new methods of making irrigation water available tend, as has been shown, merely to change the lòcale of agriculture without increasing the total acreage under the plough.

The report goes on to state that one of the essentials for real agricultural development is the increase of numbers of the rural population to provide a sufficient population for land brought within irrigation schemes.

Obstacles to Progress

The obstacles likely, in Iraq as elsewhere, to confront the realization of such development projects are not insuperable. They are connected in the first place with agricultural and technical or, more precisely, technical irrigation problems. In addition to the soil problems familiar to Middle Eastern lands, such as salinity, soil poverty, swampy lands, etc., special problems have to be solved in Iraq in connection with the nature of its water courses. The main problem in Iraq has always been that of the regulation and rational distribution of irrigation water. The violent and rapid rise in the level of the rivers in the spring, with the melting of the snows on the hills of Asia Minor, leads to heavy annual flooding of large areas in the plain country and often causes considerable damage. A further result of these periodic floods is the change in the usual direction of the streams and rivers. Almost every year sees variations in the beds of these streams, and especially of the smaller streams. The building of canals frequently promotes such deviations of rivers from their original beds, since the stream often flows more easily in the better-shaped artificial canal than in its own tortuous bed. A natural factor facilitating irrigation practices in Iraq is that the tributary canals of the Tigris system in most cases flow on a somewhat higher level than the surrounding country, which renders possible irrigation by gravity, the simplest and least expensive method. The extent to which the present cultivable area can be expanded without great outlay or effort is indicated by the highly developed ancient network of canals still visible to-day. These canals (or their traces), which may not all have been simultaneously operated, now run across land which has taken on the appearance of a steppe, although it must in the past have been the scene of flourishing cultivation. The expansion of the cultivated area in Iraq is, however, not a question of recovery of ancient canals or construction of new ones alone, but rather of the systematic maintenance of their efficiency.

Without adequate care canals rapidly become obsolete and useless. Students of Iraqi history lay special stress on the fact that the decay of Iraqi agriculture was due largely to neglect of the magnificent canal system which it inherited from a past civilization.

In recent years work has been carried out on a number of irrigation improvements in Iraq. The Hindiya Barrage, constructed in 1910, has been reconstructed. The Saglawiya, Yusufiya and Iskandria canals have been extended and reconstructed, so that a total area of 890,000 dunams can now be watered from them. Other canals have also been improved, including in particular those connected with the Diyala River system. The Kut Barrage, Iraq's most modern and biggest irrigation project, was completed in 1938 and now serves a considerable irrigated area. But the effectiveness of all these works must ultimately depend on the care exercised in the control of subsidiary canals.

Next in importance to the technical problem of irrigation is the essential need for the reform of land rights, which are to a large extent chaotic and unsettled.

This fact, together with the sparsity of population, encourages the practice of a type of primitive mobile agriculture, under which the peasant in many parts of the country moves from area to area as the fertility of each successive piece of land is exhausted. While, on the one hand, the Fellah population has no secure ownership, there are a considerable number of large landowners, holding properties of 1,000 dunams or more of irrigable land. The revision of the present unsatisfactory state of land property law is a *sine qua non* of Iraq's further progress in the domain of agriculture.

2. Settlement Capacity of Syria and the Lebanon

Conditions in the Syrian states show several points of resemblance to those obtaining in Iraq. Syria is an agrarian country, thinly populated in most parts and extensively cultivated. As in Iraq, no data other than estimates are available for the extent of the cultivable area, population density, etc. But here the estimates of land are based on repeated calculations of the authorities, particularly the Survey Department of the Government, to whose courtesy the author is indebted. Figures refer to 1935, but it does not seem that great changes have occurred since then although more recent estimates differ in regard to the extent of the cultivable and irrigable area.

Unlike Iraq, nomad tribes do not constitute a large section of the population in Syria, their numbers hardly reaching 300,000, i.e. 10 per cent. of the total number of inhabitants. The coastal zone, densely populated since antiquity, differs markedly in its economic and social structure from the eastern part of the country, which exhibits a stage of transition approaching the Iraqi level. Although well endowed with regional water supplies, Syria lacks the central irrigation waterways which dominate the cultivation possibilities in Iraq.

In view of the widely differing conditions in various parts of the country it is essential to consider, together with the general density and area figures, separate data referring to the various natural divisions of the country shown in the table below :

FIGURES FOR 1935

	Total Area (sq. kms.).	Cultivable Area (sq. kms.).	Population.	Density per sq. km. Cultivable Area.
I. Republic of Syria :				
A. Area to the West of the Euphrates and of the desert region—				
1. Damascus region	10,551	6,600	824,401	39·9
2. Central Syria .	17,074	14,050		
3. Aleppo region *.	19,288	14,350	656,516	45·7
4. Latakia region .	6,300	3,936	322,000	81·7
B. Areas across the Euphrates (Jezireh)	37,480	12,600†	209,531	16·6
C. Jebel Druse	6,800	1,600	65,465	40·8
D. Desert and steppe regions	90,846	—	—	—
Total Syrian Republic : .	188,339	53,136	2,077,813	39·2
II. Republic of Lebanon :	9,355	5,604	854,693	152·5
Total	197,694	58,740	2,932,506	49·9

* Excluding Alexandretta District, which in 1935 was still included in the total for the Aleppo Region.

† Estimate.

As will be seen, the Lebanese Republic is by far the most densely populated part of the Syrian territories. On the other hand, the Jebel Druse and the Euphrates districts fall behind the Lebanese levels ; although, when cultivable areas alone are considered, higher figures are naturally obtained. The calculations of population density are based on figures for the cultivable instead of total area, which permit comparison with other countries and give a better estimate of the additional settlement possibilities offered in Syria.

All Syrian economists are agreed that the small numbers and inadequate means of the present population of Syria prevent the development of the country's productive assets to the full.

Special stress is laid on the fact that half or less of Syria's cultivable area is at present being worked, and that only a fraction of its considerable irrigation possibilities are being used to fructify its large stretches of valuable agricultural land. Out of an estimated irrigable area of 12,000 sq. kms. barely a fifth is at present actually cultivated under irrigation. The areas mainly to be considered from the point of view of irrigation development are the plains and valleys in Central, North and North-East Syria, and the coastal plain where use could be made of the water resources of the Litani, the Orontes, the Khabur and the Euphrates, various lakes and swamps in Central Syria and smaller local springs and rivers.

In an instructive description of the water problem in Syria and the Lebanon, Mr. Soubhi Mazloum, Irrigation Engineer in Northern Syria, has given valuable details on the extent and localities of the irrigable area of both countries.[1] According to his figures, the present scope of the irrigated land comprises 250,000 ha. in Syria and 30,000 ha. in the Lebanon, in all 280,000 ha., i.e. no more than one-third of the total area that could be irrigated through exploitation of the rainwater. In addition, the tremendous possibilities of riverain irrigation must be taken into account. The total area irrigable from all sources has been computed by this expert at 1,200,000 ha. which is more than four times the area at present under irrigation. There is no need to dwell on the importance of the fact that such a tremendous area is still open to irrigation, more especially in view of the potential need for employing additional workers through the introduction of irrigated cultures as compared with dry farming. The following are Mr. Mazloum's own words :

> En Syrie, où la densité moyenne est de 8 habitants par Km² et décroit à un taux infime dans la vallée de l'Euphrate et du Khabour, le problème de la main d'œuvre se pose avec une particulière acuité ; et c'est d'ailleurs ce qui a déterminé, à juste titre, l'inscription en première ligne de l'aménagement de la vallée

[1] S. Mazloum, " Le Problème de l'Eau au Liban et en Syrie " incl. in *L'Agriculture Richesse Nationale*, Beyrouth, 1942.

de l'Oronte, où la présence d'une main d'œuvre suffisante fait espérer une exploitation rapide des terres valorisées. . . .

Toutefois, l'insuffisance de la main d'œuvre n'est pas une cause dirimante qui oblige à surseoir à tout aménagement hydraulique, dans les régions déshéritées : avec l'amélioration de l'hygiène rurale, la population du Japon a doublé en moins de 30 ans ! En Syrie, les statistiques nous manquent pour préciser le croît annuel de la population ; mais, il est permis de penser qu'en améliorant les conditions d'existence du paysan, en dirigeant avec prudence la sédentarisation des nomades et en encourageant l'exode vers les centres irrigués, provoqué par l'attrait naturel de l'eau, on parviendra à accroître, à très bref délai, l'effectif de la main d'œuvre disponible. . . .

Le journalier agricole y trouvera aussi de précieux avantages. En zone non irriguée, la main d'œuvre ordinaire n'est guère employée plus de 60 jours par an ; et les longues périodes d'inactivité qui se succèdent dans le travail des terres mettent les ouvriers journaliers dans une situation difficile qui les oblige à émigrer, pour chercher du travail en ville, ou à travailler sur les routes, si l'occasion se produit ; avec l'irrigation, les travaux sont plus réguliers et s'échelonnent tout au long de l'année, par le jeu des diverses cultures ; les ouvriers sont plus demandés et, utilisés à des cultures riches, ils sont mieux payés ; le chômage périodique de la main d'œuvre rurale est ainsi résorbé.[1]

Wide potentialities for agricultural development and settlement expansion thus exist in Syria, and their materialization will depend mainly on :

(*a*) the introduction of more advanced agricultural methods to reduce the proportion of fallow lands ;
(*b*) expansion of irrigation ;
(*c*) drainage of the marshes in the Syrian plains and in the vicinity of Damascus ;
(*d*) supply of labour necessary for the execution of the schemes under (*a*)–(*c*).

3. Other Oriental Countries

Iraq and Syria deserve pride of place in the Middle East from the point of view of unused settlement capacity. But a study of conditions in other Middle East countries leads to substantially similar conclusions.

The possibilities afforded in Transjordan are of particular interest, though here it is not easy to reach definite conclusions in the absence of many important statistics. According to the statements of the Transjordan authorities, irrigable areas are

[1] S. Mazloum, op. cit., pp. 67–8.

very limited, albeit there are still possibilities for an extension of dry farming. According to an estimate of the Director of Development in Transjordan, there might be room for a supplementary agricultural population of 100,000 to 150,000 souls. This estimate, it must be remembered, is extraordinarily conservative and disregards the experience gained, for instance, in the opening-up of landed areas and reduction of the lot viable in Palestine. For this reason it does not appear unduly optimistic to assume the possibility of a not inconsiderable rise in the agricultural absorptive capacity.

In Turkey, only 30 per cent. at the outside of the extensive cultivable area of 300,000 sq. kms. is cultivated and even that predominantly under a very extensive system.

Even in Egypt, densely populated and exploited as its cultivated area is, there exist very important projects for additional reclamation of land hitherto waste. The area which can be converted into fertile land is estimated at 12,000 sq. kms., a vast expanse compared to the present extent of the cultivable area in Egypt. At the same time, however, comprehensive measures are called for to solve the problems of saline lands and marshes and of restoring the natural properties of the soil.

For further particulars see Appendix II, where a number of development schemes are listed.

4. The Irrigation Factor

In estimating the absorptive capacity of Oriental countries, a characteristic and vital factor, viz. the paramount importance of irrigation, cannot be stressed strongly enough. Although repeatedly mentioned before, this factor requires to be treated here at greater length.

Unlike countries in the temperate zone, the agricultural potentialities of the Middle East countries are largely dominated by the fact that they include substantial territories which require the use of artificial irrigation for the achievement of their maximum yields. Irrigated agriculture means the considerable additional application of capital and labour. But in return for this there is a manifold increase in productivity and a substantial expansion of yields per unit of area even compared to those zones where irrigated cultivation has been occasionally practised but has not yet reached its optimum.

Without irrigation no cultivation is possible in the extremely arid areas lacking in natural rainfall. Where there is already a certain amount of natural precipitation, additional irrigation enables the cultivation of valuable crops with high humidity requirements which cannot otherwise be grown. Irrigation expands the range of crops, permits the cultivation of several crops per year and thus extends the agricultural season over practically the whole year.

The volume of water available is of course a primary factor in determining irrigation technique, its organization and distribution. The nature of the water supply, whether derived from surface river sources or from wells or springs is a second factor influencing the type of irrigated agriculture. Rivers, in addition to their irrigation functions, sometimes fulfil an invaluable rôle as the vehicles of fertilizing sediments, which constantly enrich the irrigated soils. The topographical structure of the land is another essential which shapes irrigation methods. Thus plain country offers the most favourable conditions, although slopes and terraces, too, are utilized to no small extent in Middle East irrigated agriculture.

Irrigation and Population Density

The peculiarities of irrigated agriculture lead to a relationship between labour applied and the unit of area basically different from that characteristic of dry farming, which employs no human labour to supply its water needs. The outstanding feature of irrigated agriculture is the high coefficient of manpower required, resulting in the far higher density of population in irrigated territories. Indeed density figures for irrigation countries are frequently many times greater than those of dry cultivation countries, as may be seen from the following table :

Density of Population subsisting on Agriculture per square kilometre of Cultivated Land [1]

Irrigated Regions.		*Non-irrigated Regions.*	
Egypt :		Poland	91
Cultivated area	497	Belgium	92
Crop area	327	Hungary	62
Palestine :		Germany	48
Northern Sharon block	288	France	45
Emek Hefer block	126	Iraq : Mosul Liwa	22
Iraq :		Syria : Aleppo Region (cultivated area)	28
Basra Liwa	284		
Baghdad Liwa	98		

[1] Figures for Palestine : *Bulletin of the Economic Research Institute*, J.A., 1939, p. 43 ; Egypt : *Statistical Yearbook*, 1937 ; Iraq : *Dowson Report* for 1930 ; other countries calculated according to *International Yearbook of Agricultural Statistics* for 1935–7.

This table illustrates the amazing differences in density of population shown by irrigated and non-irrigated zones. The relationship between the type of cultivation and population density is reciprocal in effect. A high population density necessitates more intensive agricultural forms such as are offered by irrigation economies ; a smaller population must limit itself to extensive cultivation and to the meagre ields of an extensive economy. Vice versa, intensive irrigated farming is only possible where a multitude of working hands is available and, as long as the capacity limit has not been reached, leads automatically to an increased absorption of population and also to an increasingly higher population density. The growth of population, in turn, is made possible by the larger yields per cultivation unit.

The foregoing is borne out by a reference to the figures considered to be standard for the density of the agricultural population in non-irrigated (European) territories. The average density figure of the rural population living on unirrigated land has been put at 50 per square kilometre, i.e. 1 person per 2 hectares (= 20 metric dunams). The humidity requirements of such cultivation area are supplied from the sky, thus involving no special effort on the part of man, beast, or machine as in the case of artificial irrigation. This figure for dry cultivation tallies with another assumption, according to which 5–7 hectares are taken to be the normal subsistence area for a holding where mixed farming is practised with grain as the chief item of production. Irrigated farming, however, when properly applied, needs no more than 2–3 ha. per holding. The fundamental difference between irrigated agriculture and dry cultivation from the view-point of working hands is thus to be sought in the higher labour density of the former. The additional labour requirements can be satisfied only by providing new man-power, and this extra outlay of labour and water involved in irrigated agriculture is compensated by yields which,. as a rule, exceed those of dry cultivation.

This aspect of irrigated economy may also be illustrated by a comparison of yields per unit of area. As the table on page 147 shows, yields may reach an extraordinarily high figure in irrigation zones.

Irrigated agriculture, however, if practised by primitive methods in countries at a low stage of development, cannot equal the yields obtained through the application of scientific methods in temperate countries with Western civilization. Here

AVERAGE YIELD IN KG. PER HECTARE OF WHEAT

	1936.	1937.	1938.
I. Non-irrigated crops :			
Palestine :			
General average . . .	330	560	250
Jewish settlements * . .	810	1,200	660
Turkey †	1,090	1,080	1,110
Canada †	580	470	910
England †	2,060	2,060	2,560
II. Irrigated crops :			
Egypt †	2,100	2,150	2,100
Iraq ‡ (average 1930–2) . .		1,200–1,500	
Palestine : Jewish settlements (average 1940–2) . .		2,000–3,000	

* " Yalkut " issued by Audit Union of Jewish Agric. Lab. Co-op.
† *International Yearbook of Agric. Statistics,* 1938–9.
‡ Data collected by author from Ministry of Agriculture in Baghdad.

modern agricultural science and technique as well as abundant natural precipitation have created similar and sometimes even more favourable conditions than those prevailing in the classical countries of irrigation. If, however, modern knowledge is combined with irrigation technique in the Eastern countries, results are obtained which are scarcely rivalled anywhere. To what degree the achievement of outstanding production increases is possible under these circumstances is proved by experiments made in Palestine and elsewhere with the irrigated cultivation of cereals, ground nuts, bananas and other crops suitable to climatic conditions.

The farming revenue obtained from irrigated agriculture by far exceeds returns possible from unirrigated agriculture. Conditions in Middle East countries offer ample evidence for this, as may be seen from the table on page 148.

The figures in the table would seem to lead to the conclusion that not less than 64·7 per cent. of the total value of crops (amounting in the five countries under consideration to LP.156,300,000) derives from irrigated land, although the irrigated area does not exceed 25 per cent. of the actually cultivated area.

Conditions elsewhere indicate similar developments. In California, for instance, where modern agricultural science has been linked with the intensive cultivation of irrigated crops, farming revenue per head of population is four times higher than the national average in the United States and indeed is the highest in the world.[1]

[1] C. J. Hitch, *America's Economic Strength,* Oxford University Press, 1941, p. 37.

VALUE OF CROPS IN THE MIDDLE EAST (ESTIMATES—1937)

Country.	Cultivable Area.	Cultivated Area.	Irrigated Area.	Gross Value of Crops.	Thereof on Irrigated Land.
	sq. km.	sq. km.	sq. km.	in £ million.	
Egypt	34,000	24,000	23,000	75·2	75·2
Turkey	300,000	87,000	4,000	48·2	8·1
Iraq	92,000	13,000	7,000	15·5	10·7
Syria and Lebanon* .	61,000	16,000	2,100	10·4	3·0
Palestine	12,000	9,000	400	7·0	4·0
Total	499,000	149,000	36,500	156·3	101·0

* Including the Alexandretta District.

If the irrigation factor is disregarded, the following differences in density per square kilometre are observed :

DENSITY OF RURAL POPULATION PER SQ. KM. OF CULTIVABLE LAND, 1939

Country.	Total Population as at 31 Dec., 1939.	Rural Population	Total Area.	Cultivable Area.	Rural Population per sq. km. Cultivable Area.
	in 1,000s.		in 1,000 sq. kms.		
Egypt	16,680	13,700	1,000	34	403
Turkey	17,620	14,600	768	302	48
Iraq	3,700	2,100	453	92	23
Syria and Lebanon * .	3,700	2,500	197	59	42
Palestine	1,502	800	27	12	67

* Excluding the Alexandretta District.

5. CONCLUSIONS

When investigating the absorptive capacity of an area in relation to the given natural conditions, it must be borne in mind that the density of population is not a rigid concept but a fluctuating index. In all modern definitions of the population capacity of a country, great stress is laid on the elastic character of the latter, as otherwise one might overlook the peculiar local conditions as well as changes and variations which continue even during the very settlement of a country. This emphasis on the relative value of any strict formula for the absorptive capacity of a country derives from the experience of countries that are already densely populated, in which prognoses of "saturation points" have repeatedly proved to be incorrect. The reason for this lies in the frequent innovations which modify, sometimes in an exceedingly brief period, the conditions that serve as a point of issue for the whole question. In countries as far from any theoretical saturation point as most of the lands of the Orient the judgment of the absorptive capacity is far less complicated. The technical innovations of our time, moreover, are of particular benefit to those very areas the opening-up of which was formerly fraught with great difficulties (finding of subsoil water, transport and communication problems, storage difficulties, etc.). The experience in making the utmost use of all technical facilities already gained in one country, namely Palestine, concerning which all prognoses of absorptive capacity have proved inaccurate, has astonished all experts. It has further taught that the prerequisites for successful agricultural settlement consist to a very large degree in an increase in density of the whole population, particularly of urban settlements, which are of vital importance as customers for the increased output. Naturally this is not a process that can be commenced and completed from one day to the next. The development of trade, industry, public services and transport must go hand in hand with that of agriculture.

Bearing this in mind, we shall finally summarize our computations of the potential agricultural capacity as follows:

The area on which irrigated farming can be practised in the Middle East may be estimated at approximately 132,000 sq. kms. in Iraq, Syria and the Lebanon, Palestine, Transjordan, Turkey and Egypt. Of this at present only 37,000 sq. kms. are cultivated under irrigation, in many cases by primitive and wasteful methods; there remain about 95,000 sq. kms. not yet irrigated. Some countries show percentages of irrigated land considerably lower than might be expected. Thus, for instance, in Iraq, out of an estimated irrigable area of 51,000 sq. kms. only 7,000 sq. kms. are under irrigation. In Palestine, out of 4,000 sq. kms., 400 sq. kms. are actually irrigated.

The average agricultural density of population per sq. km.

of irrigable land will not be too highly computed at 200. If the whole of the Middle East irrigable but not yet irrigated area is considered, this would indicate room for an additional population of 19,000,000. If for the purposes of a conservative estimate we assume that of the 95,000 sq. kms. of Middle East irrigable but unirrigated land more than a third is worked under extensive cultivation and carries a population of 80 per square kilometre, the additional population figure might be computed at about 16,400,000.

On the other hand, we have not taken into consideration that of the unirrigable but cultivable lands of the Middle East a substantial part (some 257,000 sq. kms.) is still uncultivated.

Even at the lowest estimate, with a density figure of only 50 per square kilometre, the Middle East's unirrigable but cultivable land would provide room for an additional population of 12,850,000 and together with the area of irrigation, the Middle East's capacity for additional agricultural population may be reckoned at nearly 30,000,000.

But it should again be stressed that these figures cannot be taken as the only criterion for the approach to the question of settlement. The total population capacity of the Middle Eastern countries may greatly exceed the figures listed above or, on the other hand, remain far below the limit mentioned here.

The crux of this issue turns on the density of population in relation to *the material and cultural stage of development* they have reached. A most illuminating lesson in this respect is provided by the conditions prevailing in those very countries in ancient times. A comparison of past and present shows that there can be no question of any constant capacity of those countries, which in ancient times maintained a population many times larger than the present one, for supporting human beings. As to the manner in which the population of the Orient in antiquity was in a position to reach so high a grade of civilization, it is explained by noted scholars on good grounds that a most important and possibly a decisive factor in the blossoming of these countries was the pressure of population felt in them. The high density of population which, according to modern ideas, would amount to over-population and could not be mitigated by emigration in view of the natural barriers formed by the desert, generated the will and impetus to surmount the existent obstacles apparently set by nature, and to develop ways of achieving a powerful establishment and extension of the political and economic frame.

The increase of population pressure in modern times which, as a result of post-war regrouping of nations and states, can be clearly felt in all potential settlement countries, has as yet touched the countries of the Middle East to but a limited degree. There can be no doubt that, in any preparations to solve the world's land settlement problems on a large scale, the existence of extensive under-population in the Middle East must no longer be ignored. The countries of the Middle East are favoured in respect of soil and climate ; once their resources in this regard are fully exploited, those countries will be able to convert their lands, which were famous for fertility in ancient times, into a new world-centre for the production of valuable agrarian commodities. The commodities, if properly marketed, will enable them to balance the capital imports necessary for economic development. Palestine, as well as certain other countries, has shown that the economic problems involved, intricate as they are, can nevertheless be mastered.

APPENDIX II

To convey an idea of the range of possible large-scale development schemes, a list of individual projects for execution by Governments or other public bodies is given below. This list lays no claim whatever to being exhaustive. Its sole purpose is to indicate the ample opportunities for inaugurating long-term and short-term projects of development and of public works in the Middle East countries. It is obvious that in each case research will have to be undertaken on the spot by experts, with a view to determining the technical and financial requirements involved.

List of Development Schemes

Egypt

I. Hydro-electrical schemes :
   (*a*) Generation of electricity by using the falling water at the Aswan Dam, to be coupled with the establishment of a plant for the production of artificial manure ;
   (*b*) Kattara Depression project, which proposes to make use of the difference in level between the Mediterranean and the Kattara Depression by the construction of a canal from the coast to the depression in the Western desert ;
   (*c*) Assiut Barrage scheme.

II. Extensive plans for modernizing and expanding the Egyptian road system, which is very poor at present.

III. Execution of a national scheme for the supply of water to Egyptian villages.

IV. Inauguration of national schemes of housing, hospitalization and projects for the construction of public buildings.

V. Extension of the cultivated area by large-scale reclamation and irrigation works.

According to Mr. A. E. Crouchley, a close observer of modern trends in Egyptian agriculture, prospects in this vital sphere present the following picture :

The rapidly proceeding conversion of basin land in Upper Egypt to perennial irrigation will add, in round figures, a further

1,000,000 Feddans of summer cultivation, and a correspondingly increased area of potential cotton production.

In the second place it is necessary to consider other big storage reservoirs and works on the Upper Nile. Nile control, far from being completed, may be said scarcely to have begun. As long as there is an enormous quantity of water running to waste or lost through evaporation, Nile control must be considered incomplete. Plans have already been sketched out for a whole series of works going back as far as the sources of the Nile and designed to bring the whole of that mighty river under the eventual control of the irrigation engineer.

Increased supplies of water will be required for the conversion and reclamation of over 1,000,000 Feddans in Upper Egypt, the reclamation of over 2,000,000 Feddans of waste land in Lower Egypt, the extension of the area under rice, the improvement of the irrigation facilities in Lower Egypt and the provision of water for the early sowing of a large Nile maize crop. It is estimated that the water at present available in the Aswan and Gebel Awlia reservoirs is not more than one-half the quantity which will ultimately be required for these different schemes of development.

Even more acute, perhaps, is the problem of drainage. The Government has realized that it has a duty in this respect, and is providing deep main drains with powerful pumps to maintain the water at a low level. But these main ditches, to be effective, need to be linked up with an infinity of secondary and tertiary ditches covering the entire area to be served. The drainage system, to be effective, must be organized over the whole area on a single co-ordinated plan in which each farmer has his place. Yet many of the latter lack the capital for such expensive operations. Further, the provision of open drains is very wasteful, in the sense that they may take up as much as 10 per cent. of the cultivated area. In the case of many of the smaller cultivators an open drain, even a small one, running along their strip would take up the whole of their land. The solution may eventually be found by the provision of drains consisting of covered pipes, laid underground at a suitable depth and arranged on a suitably graded slope so that they may catch the subsoil water and run it off into the drainage canals. (Cp. A. E. Crouchley, *The Economic Development of Modern Egypt*, 1938, pp. 241 ff.)

Iraq

I. The principal measures in the sphere of land survey, settlement, registration and exploitation are according to the proposals of Sir Ernest Dowson :

(*a*) execution of a combined programme of cadastral survey, of settlement of rights to land, and of land valuation ;

(*b*) proper utilization and maintenance of existing and, on a country-wide scale, construction of new works —storage reservoirs, flood embankments, delivery and drainage channels, regulators.

II. The projects enumerated under (*a*) to (*c*) below were confirmed by the Iraqi Cabinet immediately before the outbreak of the present war :

(*a*) one scheme aiming at the construction of 5,000 kms. of roads all over the country, of a railway bridge for Baghdad, and a series of public works throughout the country ;

(*b*) another referring to the carrying out of the Habbaniyah flood relief scheme, designed to divert the flood waters of the Euphrates into the vast Habbaniyah Lake near the new R.A.F. base at Sinel-Dhibban. (The scheme was prepared by the Iraqi Government with the assistance of the consulting engineers, Messrs. Coode, Wilson, Mitchell, and Vaughan Lee, London, and provides, amongst others, for an inlet regulator-equipped canal to receive the flood waters when the Euphrates is high, and a similar outlet canal to return the water to the river when levels fall.)

(*c*) A flood relief scheme for the Tigris has been worked out, apart from projects for remedying bed erosion in the Euphrates River downstream from Hindiyah Barrage, Hillah. Erosion is progressing at an alarming rate, advancing upstream and threatening the existent barrages themselves.

(*d*) Large scale housing and hospitalization schemes, which are particularly urgent in the rural regions of Iraq.

(*e*) The setting up of hydro-electrical stations to promote farming.

PALESTINE

Among the outstanding projects mention must be made of—

I. Plans for the utilization of the available river-water and run-off rain-water in those regions, which at present consist of uncultivable or non-irrigable lands. The project of generating electricity for irrigation purposes by means of a sea-water canal leading to the Jordan Depression constitutes an important feature of these schemes.

II. Large housing and building schemes. A cautiously calculated programme of housing and building (public works included) arrived at a total of £30 million solely to cover the needs of the present Jewish population.

III. Extension of the existent industrial production through improved utilization of the industrial raw materials available in the country (Dead Sea deposits, refining of by-products, etc.).

IV. Systematic anti-erosion work, to be undertaken in conjunction with afforestation schemes, removal of stones and the extension of the cultivated area throughout the country.

SYRIA AND LEBANON

I. Numerous projects exist for the utilization of the surface water resources of the coastal plain and the principal rivers of the inland.

The following are the main water resources on which some of the major riverain irrigation schemes have been based : The Euphrates, Khabour, Orontes, Yammunah Lake, and the Litani.

II. A national scheme of housing and sanitation in the villages.

III. Anti-erosion and afforestation measures.

IV. Slum-clearing and building schemes.

APPENDIX III

THE EFFECT OF THE WAR ON POST-WAR FINANCE IN THE MIDDLE EAST

When the preceding lines were written there were no clear indications as to the probable effects of the war on national income, public finances, price relations, capital import, etc. Even now nothing definite can be said, but certain trends are already visible, and it may even be possible to forsee a number of lasting effects.

There can be no doubt that the inflationary features which are so conspicuous a phenomenon in the sphere of Middle Eastern prices and finance to-day are of more than ephemeral importance. Yet it would be unwise, as we shall see, to overrate their significance and to predict a complete and permanent reversal of pre-war values.

It would therefore be helpful to indicate briefly the character of inflation in the Middle East. What the countries of the Middle East have experienced, especially from the second half of the war onwards, is in effect an inflation of prices accompanied by an expansion of note circulation and bank deposits. The usual causes of a genuine inflation, such as were found to have been at the bottom of the "galloping" inflation in Europe after the last war, are definitely absent in the case before us. No government deficit has required to be covered by central bank advances, nor has any serious flight of capital been observed. There have, to be sure, been "investments" in gold or other stable values, yet on the whole on a fairly limited scale. The main reason for the price increase is, of course, to be sought in the large influx of money, i.e. purchasing power, into Middle Eastern countries through the Allied Forces. The latter's combined military expenditure in Egypt, Palestine, Iraq, Syria, the Lebanon, Iran, and the Sudan may be estimated to have reached roughly £500 million by the end of 1944. This would mean a military expenditure of about £11 per head of the Middle Eastern population. The total military expenditure within the individual countries concerned has not been in proportion to their size and population. Egypt and Palestine rank first, but it goes without saying that in countries where the national *per capita* income in peacetime is in the neighbourhood of £10, an additional purchasing power of even a few pounds per head per year is apt considerably to affect the price level, more particularly when the volume of goods, both local and foreign, at the disposal of civilian consumers is being drastically curtailed at the same time. The table below shows the various indices prevailing in 1943.

INDICES IN DECEMBER, 1943

(Base: August, 1939, or Average 1938/39 = 100)

	Egypt.	Palestine.	Syria and the Lebanon.	Iraq.	Turkey.
Currency	467	595	811	809	316
Bank Deposits . .	529	275	790	789	148 (1942)
Wholesale Prices .	293	341	901	636	473
Cost of Living . .	257	230	500	405	340

However, the facts mentioned above are not enough to permit an appreciation of the lasting changes that have occurred within the income structure of the populations concerned. As far as we can judge, there have been no decisive shifts in either the earning or the consumption powers of the *bulk* of the populations in the Middle East. All of them, the Jewish community of Palestine excepted, are preponderantly rural. A glance at the price index reveals that prices of agrarian products have risen most and, while it is certain that the entire rise has not gone into the farmer's pocket, the rural population as a whole may safely be assumed to have succeeded in at the least maintaining its pre-war position. In procuring the necessaries of life, the agricultural producer has the advantage of offering goods in exchange the value of which has grown more than the value of the commodities needed by him. Calculations of national income bear out this state of affairs. A recent investigation into the national income of Palestine has shown that the nominal rise in the income of agricultural producers has been remarkable.

But this does not affect the position as described in the foregoing chapters. A *per capita* income of £75 in 1944 is, in terms of real income, no more than one of £25 before the war, if both are the equivalent of, say, three tons of wheat. The same holds good with regard to the inflated incomes of other sections of the population. The two main questions are therefore :

(*a*) whether a deflationary movement may be anticipated which, apart from its other concomitants, would reduce price levels more or less to pre-war standards ; and

(*b*) whether a substantial part of the national purchasing power that has accrued to the Middle East would be available for purposes of future investment.

As to the first question it appears, at any rate with respect to Palestine and Egypt, that an adjustment of prices to the pre-war level or at least to the level of the Western Sterling Block is feasible and, in fact, aspired to in responsible quarters and by the Authorities. In the case of the other Middle Eastern countries, the connection between their currencies and the pound sterling will tend to favour an adjustment to pre-war standards although, because of the far higher rise in Oriental indices as compared with Western, more drastic measures may prove necessary, which may involve temporary hardships to the populations concerned.

As regards the second question, a not inconsiderable part of the imported purchasing power has accumulated in the form of sterling balances.

The foreign sterling balances accumulating in London are unquestionably a problem of great magnitude ; by the end of 1944 they will amount to some £3,000 million. The share of the Middle Eastern countries in this amount may ultimately reach the £600 million mark. The fact that these balances have sprung in the main from wartime necessity (mostly supplies to the British Army) may justify a solution that is not entirely along orthodox lines. The repatriation of abnormal war balances is one of the major post-war problems in the economic and financial sphere, and as such has played a not inconsiderable part in the discussions of the Bretton Woods Conference. Countries with large claims on Great Britain will be able to obtain satisfaction only if they agree to accept payment in goods, even though the latter may be bought cheaper elsewhere. The Oriental countries will no doubt be prepared to accept goods in exchange for their claims, provided prices are not excessive. For during the war years an enormous consumption power has accumulated there and, together with the requirements arising from the implementation of long-term development schemes, will more than suffice to absorb vast quantities of goods and thus help to liquidate within a comparatively short period the problem of the sterling balances. The difficulty would appear to be rather on the supply side. Will Great Britain produce enough to cover the needs of the holders of sterling balances in addition to her own? An answer to this question cannot be given as long as the demands of war economy take pride of place. It seems that the solution must be sought in the proper organization and handling of the goods supply to the creditor countries, a task which will extend over a number of years. The measure, suggested in some quarters, of reducing the amount of indebtedness by depreciating Oriental currencies would fail to achieve its object, for the following two reasons: In the first place, the balances owned by Middle Eastern countries are mainly in pounds sterling and would hence not be affected by a devaluation of the local Oriental currencies. Besides, Oriental people are very sensitive to manipulations of currency. The dangers involved in risking a loss of public confidence by changing the firmly established relation between the Oriental currencies and the pound sterling is surely a factor that cannot very well be ignored in fixing British financial policy.

In any case, the sterling assets are liable to contribute materially towards a solution of the problem of post-war finance in the Middle East. All that is needed would be a genuine preparedness on both sides: on the part of the creditor to enter into a long-term agreement—and on that of the debtor to meet his obligations.

Another development, and one which has aroused general attention, also has a strong bearing on the financial post-war problems of our region. The war years have witnessed an enormous revival of interest in the oil resources of the Middle East. As regards geographical position, the Middle East belongs to the favoured oil regions of the world. Furthermore, according to experience hitherto, the drilling of new oil wells presents no particular technical difficulties in this area. Iran heads Middle Eastern countries in oil production. In 1940 the quantity of oil extracted within her confines amounted to 78 million barrels; which made this country the fourth in the list of oil-producing lands. Iraq occupies the eighth place, but her resources are not yet fully developed. The coastal and border areas of the

Arab Peninsula also possess promising sources of this precious fluid, and there are signs that borings in Syria and Palestine will likewise be successful.

There can be no doubt that from the viewpoint of the finance of reconstruction and development in the Middle East the presence of oil, together with its prospective extraction and refining, is of paramount importance. Oil experts have estimated the potential oil production within this area at between 70 and 100 million tons per annum. At a price of £2 per ton this would mean an annual income of from £140 to £200 million. This vast sum would partly be spent in the Middle East region in the form of royalties, wages, purchases of local goods, etc. An amount of this order of magnitude must of necessity play a decisive rôle in the finance and execution of other development projects, provided local governments seriously intend to spend their revenues on such plans. It is not possible to give detailed calculations as to potential revenues, for the production of oil in the countries concerned is not sufficiently advanced to permit such an estimate; nor are the negotiations regarding concessions, etc., definitely concluded in every case. Yet the amounts involved are such that no far-sighted policy of reconstruction can afford to ignore them.

INDEX

Agricultural innovations, Palestine, 103–5
— produce, output and consumption, 62
— production, estimate for 1962, 67–9
— — how arrived at, 43
— — in International Prices, table, 44–5
— productivity, means of raising, 55 ff., 79, 101
— — per earner, 44–5, 46–7
— — per land unit, 47
— schools, 119
Agriculture, diversity of conditions, 101
— in Egypt, 26–9
— in Iraq, 35–8
— irrigated and dry, compared, 146
— mobile, 37, 140
— planning of capital investment, 101–8
America, and foreign credits, 98–9
Antiquity, condition of Middle East in, 134–5
Arab population, in 1962, 116
Assiut Barrage scheme, 152
Aswan Dam, 152

Banks, and interest rates, 79
Birth-rate, high, in Middle East, 8
— statistics, 9
Births, surplus, 9
Building investments, industrial, 77
Bulgaria, egg production in, 107–8
Butler, H., quoted, 4

Cairo, population, 12–13
California, farming revenue per head, 147
Canals, irrigation, 139
Capital and income, relation between, 91–2
— how to be found, 98
— importance of, 90
Capital, proportion of foreign to local, in Egypt, 96
— provision of internal, in Egypt, 99–100
Capital investment, foreign, in Turkey, 96
— — future rôle of, 97–160
— — in Egypt, 92
— — in Palestine, 94
— — in past, 95–7
— — low level of, 97
— — planned, in agriculture, 101–8
— — — in industry, 108–10
Cattle, improved types, 105–6
Civilization, ancient, factors producing, 150
Cleland, W., quoted, 31
Clothing, expenditure on, 73–4
— of Fellahin, 26
Consumption, fields for increase of, 112
Co-operation, in Palestine, 118–19
Cotton, 29, 106
Crop yields, statistics, 148
Crouchley, A. E., 152–3
Customs union, 122–8
Cyprus, agricultural conditions, 41

Dairying, in Egypt, 106
Dates, prices, 43
Death-rate, in Egypt, 30–1
— statistics, 9
Density of population, 134
— — and irrigation, 145–8
— — fluctuating character of, 148–9
— — in Iraq, 137
— — in Syria, 141
— — rural, 148
— — urban, importance of increased, 149
Density of settlement, in Palestine, 118
Development schemes, Egypt, 152–3
— — Iraq, 154
— — Palestine, 155

Development schemes, Syria, 155
— — tasks of regional bodies, 113
Dowson, Sir E., quoted, 37, 154
Drainage, in Egypt, 153

Earners, agricultural, in 1962, 68
— male, numbers of, 44–5, 46
— proportions to population, 51
Economic data, comparative, 126
— life, and federation, 122–8
— — uniformity of, 122–3
Education, in Egypt, 32–3
Egypt, agriculture, 26–9
— area, 23–4
— capital investment, 92
— crop area, 25
— density, 24–5
— development schemes, 152–3
— education, 32–3
— health, 29–32
— industrial development, 33–4
— needs for agricultural development, 105–6
— population, 15, 24–5
— provision of internal capital, 99–100
— settlement potentialities, 144
— standard of living, 29–31
Egyptian Industrialists' Association, 109
Elasticity, Income, 72
Engel's Law, 70–1
Expectation of life, 13
Expenditure, State, *per capita*, 21
Exports, agricultural, 60–1
— and population, 18
— Egyptian, 29
— invisible, 18

Family budgets, 47
Farm equipment, investment required for, 104
Federation, possibilities, 122–8
Feis, M., 98–9
Floods, 139
Food consumption, actual, in Egypt, 59
— — rural, actual and optimum, 58
— expenditure, proportion to income, 70–2

Habbaniyah flood relief scheme, 154
Health, in Egypt, 31–2
Household goods, consumption capacity for, 73
Housing, 39
— consumption capacity for, 75–8
— of Fellahin, 26
Hussein, King, 116

Imports, and exports, comparative, 127
— — Palestinian, 125
— local competition with, 81–3
Income and capital, relation between, 91–2
Income, National, 7
— — and occupational structure, 16–17
— — conditions for increase of, 17 ff.
— — per head of population, 14, 18, 21
— Real, distribution *per capita*, 53
— — need for redistribution, 53
— — need of increase *per capita*, 53–4
Incomes, average, purchasing power of, 17
India, population problem, 15–16
Industrial goods, assumed rise in consumption, 78
— productivity, per head, 49
— workers, estimated increase, 83–4
Industrialization, in Egypt, 33–4
— in Iraq, 38
— insufficiency of, 55
— prospects of, 69–72
Industry, planning of capital investment in, 108–10
Infant mortality, in Egypt, 30
Innovations, agricultural, in Palestine, 103–5
Interest rate, 79–80
International co-operation, financial, 110–14
— Price, 42
— Unit, defined, 17 *n.*, 42
Investment, average, per worker, in agriculture and industry, 48
See also Capital
Iraq, 34–8
— development schemes, 154

Iraq, land surface classification, 137
— population deficiency, 138–9
— settlement potentialities, 136–40
Irrigation, 63–4, 144–8, 149
— in Iraq, 136–7, 139
— in Palestine, 118
— in Syria, 105, 142

Ja'far Pasha al Askari, 138
Japan, population problem, 15
Jewish immigration, in Palestine, 115–17

Kattara Depression project, 152
Kut Barrage, 140

Labour organization, in Palestine, 120–1
— shortage, agricultural, in Iraq, 65
— — — possible, in Egypt, 66
Land ownership, distribution in Egypt, 28
— — in Iraq, 35–6, 140
— surface, Iraq, classification, 137
— tenure, 39–40
— utilization, 62–4
— — statistics, 63
Landed property, breaking up of, in Egypt, 27
Lawrence, T. E., quoted, 116
Lebanon, agricultural conditions, 40–1
— economic position, 123–4
See also Syria
Livestock, actual and required numbers, in U.S.A., 57
— improvement, in Palestine, 118
Living space, insufficiency of, 134

Machinery imports, 21
Manufactured goods, capacity for increasing consumption, 70
Mazloum, Soubhi, quoted, 142–3.
Middle East Supply Centre, 112
Milk output, 106
Motor vehicles, 21, 85

Natural resources, 18–20
New economic order, principles, 5
Nile control, 153
Nutrition policy requirements, British, 57
— — — Middle East, 57 ff., 131
— — — U.S.A., 56–7
— standards, 39

Occupational shift, 16–17
Oil, 19–20, 38
Oranges, prices, 43 *n.*
Output, industrial, *see* Productivity
Over-population, 10, 14 ff.

Palestine, agricultural conditions, 41, 117–19
— and customs union, 123–5
— capital investment in, 94
— development schemes, 155
— imports and exports, 125
— industry, 119–21
— Jewish settlement, 115–17
— needs for agricultural development, 102–5
— rapid development, 21
— recent development, 115
Peasants, programme for improvement of standard of living, 130
Planning, aims of, 54
— importance of, 2
— preparation for, 6–7
— purpose of, 3–4, 129
Planning, quoted, 111–12
Population, additional, possible, 63–4, 150
— agricultural, possible additional, 63–4
— density, *see* Density
— growth of, 1–2
— — since 1800, 10
— increase, in Egypt, 10, 25
— of large towns, 11
— policy, 20–1
— potential growth, 64–5
— problem, factors determining, 9
— tendencies, 13
— urban proportion, 12
— — — in Egypt, 27
Poultry farming, in Balkans, 107–8
Price ratio, agricultural and industrial, change in, 66–9

Primary products, need to raise exchange value, 54
Producers' goods industries, in Palestine, 120–1
Productivity, agricultural, per family, in 1962, 69
— — per head, 44–5
— — per land unit, 47
— industrial, per head, 49–51
Public services, need for development, 54

Railways, 21, 85
— investments in, 93
Rents, in Egypt, 27–9
— of farms, 80
Revenue, per head, 21
Rotation of crops, improved, 117

Secondary occupations, earners and incomes, 88
Self-sufficiency, agricultural, 61–2
Services, increased demand for, 85
Settlement potentialities, Egypt, 144
— — Iraq, 136–40
— — Syria and Lebanon, 140–3
— — Transjordan, 143–4
— — Turkey, 144
Standard of living, and population, 15–16
— — effects of industrialization, 86–9
— — how improvable, 16 ff., 52 ff., 130
— — in Egypt, 26, 29–33
Switzerland, 18
Syria, agricultural conditions, 40
— area and density statistics, 141
— development schemes, 155
Syria, industrialization and imports, 83
— irrigation, 105
— needs for agricultural development, 105
— settlement potentialities, 140–3

Taxation, in Egypt, 100
Technical progress, 19, 20
Tertiary occupations, earners and incomes, 88
— — expected development, 85–6
Tourist industry, 20
Training of workers, 84
Transjordan, settlement potentialities, 143–4
Transport development, 85–6
Tribal settlement, in Iraq, 37
Turkey, agricultural conditions, 41
— foreign capital in, 96
— industrialization and imports, 83
— settlement potentialities, 144

Unemployment, 132
Urbanization, in Egypt, 26–7

Wage rates, anticipated increase, 87–8
Wages, industrial, 50
— — in Egypt, 33–4
War industries, in Palestine, 120
Water resources, sub-surface, 118
Wheat, improved types, 103–5
— irrigated and non-irrigated, yield per unit area, 147
Winant, W., quoted, 3
Workers, increased political importance, 14
— organization of, in Palestine, 120, 121

For Product Safety Concerns and Information please contact our EU representative GPSR@taylorandfrancis.com
Taylor & Francis Verlag GmbH, Kaufingerstraße 24, 80331 München, Germany

www.ingramcontent.com/pod-product-compliance
Ingram Content Group UK Ltd.
Pitfield, Milton Keynes, MK11 3LW, UK
UKHW022156190926
475702UK00003B/62
* 9 7 8 0 4 1 5 1 7 5 2 5 8 *